GW00859243

How to ACE the Leaving Certificate

Joe McCormack

Acknowledgements

This book is dedicated to the following for their interest, expertise and encouragement during this process:

My Family:
Joe and Eileen McCormack.
Mary Rose, Alan, Evan and Rebecca Staunton.

My Support Network:
Aedín Tynan, Ephrem Feeley, Claire O'Rourke, Val Treacy, Kevin Murphy, Phil Dunning (R.I.P) and Mary (Molly) McCormack (R.I.P.).

My Educational and Professional Network:
Ms. Anne Gray and Mr. Tomas Korintus (A&J Print), Ms. Caroline Twomey (Atlantic Way Editing and Proofreading), Mr. Liam Birkett, Ms. Emily Bollard, Ms. Emily White, Ms. Paula Bhreathnach, Ms. Aisling Clery and Mr. Steven O'Connor (Webmarket.ie).

Cover Design, Typesetting: A & J Print Ltd.
Typeset in Minion Pro and Myriad Pro
Edited by: Ms. Caroline Twomey (AWEP)
Presented by: Mr. Joe McCormack (B.A., H.Dip.Ed, H.Dip.IT)

ISBN-13:978-1724480507
ISBN-10:1724480502
www.acesolutionbooks.com
First Edition Published November 2017
© Joe McCormack 2017

Printed by: A & J Print Ltd,
Greenpark, Dunshaughlin, Co. Meath.

All rights reserved. No part of this publication may be reproduced, stored in a retrieval system, or transmitted in any form or by any means, electronic, mechanical, photocopying, recording or otherwise without prior written permission of the publisher.

Contents

Preface

Today, the final exam at the end of Secondary School is the main gateway to further education, training, and jobs in Ireland. With an enhanced level of completion, the importance of this exam has come sharply into focus. The emphasis is now swaying towards continuous assessment; you, as a student, have an opportunity to develop, enhance and show off your skills during the year and work done will be aggregated towards your final mark. I am sure you would prefer to have some marks in the bag heading into the final exam as opposed to having all the emphasis on one day, similar to what is currently happening in subjects like History, Construction Studies and Geography for example. Spreading the risk is wise, especially as things can go wrong on the day; you could be unlucky with your paper, have a personal problem, or even feel unwell.

While a model of continuous assessment is welcomed, I feel that the terminal exam is, and will continue to be, the fairest and most efficient way to differentiate students in preparation for third level education. The brilliant thing about the Leaving Certificate final exam is that everyone is on the one level playing field. The standard of integrity of the State Exams Commission (SEC) is extremely high, therefore grades achieved by students are genuine and earned. I have always been fascinated with how students prepare, cope with, react to and write final exams. I am intrigued how we, as teachers and parents, can help you improve your knowledge and develop your skills to help you achieve better results.

Every year a new group of enthusiastic students arrive into sixth year thinking "How Can I ACE the Leaving Cert?" This book focuses on providing essential advice and techniques that will help you do exactly that. It will discuss studying in the most efficient way, preparing for your mocks, the final lead up, just before the exams, the exam hall itself, and of course, writing the paper. This book will also give an insight into nutrition and advice for your parents, so that they can help you in the best way possible. It is natural for anxiety levels to elevate as the exams approach and you may even find you can't breathe properly or the worry causes butterflies in your stomach. The advantage of knowing what to expect and being seriously prepared is that you can relax and feel confident as you start your exams. This book will provide loads of information that will build your confidence and settle those nerves. You can open it on any chapter depending on what stage of the year you are at.

Along with imparting my own practical knowledge, advice lists and examples, I have also enlisted the help of current sixth years and former students who have just completed their exams. They have advised me on what they would have liked to have in place, the pitfalls and what worked and didn't work for them. The survey results from the sixty-strong cohort in Chapter Nine is a very interesting read. On my part, I have attended many conferences and seminars, have reviewed many videos, presentations and documents, and handpicked the most relevant facts for you. Wrapped together, I hope each page will inspire and give you the confidence to achieve your wildest Educational dreams, and above all 'ACE' the Leaving Cert.

ACE Inspirational Quotes

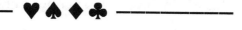

"You've got to take responsibility and
do everything in your power to get results"
Steven Gerrard.

"There's a spark in you. You just gotta
ignite the light and let it shine"
Katy Perry.

Chapter 1:

My 'Top Forty' Smart Ways to Study

So Many Ways to Study

When your teacher asks you to study something or your parents say, "go and do a bit of study", what are you thinking? Or more importantly, what do you actually go and do?

What is study? I believe study is the way a person learns in their own unique way and that every single individual does so differently. A starting point is to understand that you and your best friend probably study and learn in totally different ways. It is up to you to figure out the ways in which your mind learns and then to develop those learning styles to the best of your ability. This will involve trying various methods to see which ones suit you.

"I stand upon my desk to remind myself that we must constantly look at things in a different way"

John Keating (The Dead Poet's Society)

There is a misconception out there among some parents and students that study is simply reading your textbook. There are infinite ways an individual can study and learn including: listening, teaching, talking, revision, highlighting, reading, underlining, note taking, summarising, helping others etc. Many of these methods will be discussed throughout this book so it might be an idea, when you come across one you like, to take note and test it out to see if it suits you. By trialling different ways of studying, you will soon figure out which ones are most beneficial to you. The more ways of learning you can tap into, the higher the likelihood is of 'ACE-ing' your exams.

With so many distractions these days, it has become more difficult to knuckle down to learning. To succeed though, you must try and set aside study time each night. If you are reading this book, you more than likely have a desire to succeed and know in your heart, that the time will come when some serious planning, preparation and study will be required to achieve the grades you need. Studying each subject requires different approaches and skills, and tapping into the knowledge of your subject teacher is a useful starting point, asking them the best way to prepare in their subject. Be sure to write down what each teacher says, as good advice should always be noted, otherwise it will be lost. Remember that each teacher is an expert in their own subject area, so make sure to take advantage of their knowledge and experience.

Let's get Motivated

Are you struggling for motivation at the moment? Having high motivation levels is an important element of getting any task completed. The first thing to realise is that you can achieve any goal by discovering ways to motivate and drive yourself on. Try to accept other people and the skills that they have, remembering that you have talents that they may not possess. Wanting to be like your peers too much will probably not be that beneficial to you. You are unique, with so many different, amazing qualities and when you find your focus, you will achieve great things too.

The way we converse can sometimes reflect our motivation levels and can also increase them intrinsically, without us even knowing. Highly motivated individuals will use words like 'could', 'will', 'may', 'like to' as opposed to 'must', 'won't', 'can't' and 'need to'. Writing, considering and repeating positive sentences out loud can improve motivation and reset a positive mind-set. Here are some examples of these sentences in the context of your final year. You should re-write these to reflect your own current situation and mind-set.

- ♣ I want to start preparing myself for the upcoming exams.

- ♣ I need to put a structured timetable in place.

- ♣ I'd like to get into University after school.

5

♣ I should get my head in the books this weekend.

♣ I have to start working hard to reach my short term goals.

♣ I can achieve whatever I want through hard work.

♣ I will deliver brilliant exam scripts in this year's Leaving Cert.

♣ I am going to set up a little study group.

♣ I know that I have plenty of ability.

♣ I am a force to be reckoned with.

Hearing about the study habits of others on Instagram or Facebook can be a positive thing. Instead of feeling bad about not being highly driven, use it to motivate yourself. The fact that there is someone out there competing against you, who wants your college place, should get you going and make you more determined. Another motivating factor in this final year is its length. The length of sixth year is just nine months, so you only really need to raise your game for that short period. Do you fancy repeating somewhere while your friends head off to college or employment or how does re-studying everything in a repeat year sound? Not too appealing I would imagine. Again, don't ignore these thoughts; instead use them to inspire yourself. It's a nice idea to list out motivations on the back of your school journal, having a glance at them whenever you find yourself losing interest in your work.

Accept the Things I Cannot Change

Upon reaching the Christmas break, you are roughly half way through the year so you need to ask yourself at that point, "Am I on track to deliver a performance when the big day arrives?" Being on holidays at Christmas normally serves as a re-motivator to keep going or get back on track. Guilt, even though it is not a pleasant emotion, can be a positive force to give you that push forward you need. Ask yourself, "Will I feel better or worse if I do absolutely nothing over the next week?" It is worth remembering that you cannot change the past and it shouldn't limit you either. I always remind my students that you can only shape your future through present actions. The prayer of serenity comes to mind here:

"Accepting the things I cannot change
courage to change the things I can,
and the wisdom to know the difference"

Having a bad day can unfortunately commence a negative thought process: "I'll drop down to pass or foundation to concentrate on other subjects". You need to guard against one lapse destroying your motivation for a subject. A bad day is not a bad week and this is a long-term project.

If things are not progressing well; your grades, performance and teachers' feelings are three pointers guiding any decision on a potential movement of level. It is normal to have difficulty getting started sometimes; it's not always going to be perfect. You may be in a bad humour or just not feeling positive on study nights, facing into certain subjects. Perseverance and doggedness are two key features of success. You will get there if you keep trying and will achieve what you want if you stick at it.

In this book, I will give you a myriad of specific pieces of advice. Alongside your subject teacher's expertise, this will hopefully be the key to you unlocking the exam door – the magical recipe for success, the winning hand, the full house. At a minimum; you will have a solid plan you can work to, be more informed about studying efficiently, be more organised, and most importantly, be poised to deliver the best quality exam script you can. To be successful in any realm of life-a good plan is necessary. I will give you all the details for creating this plan in Chapter Two.

Super Organisation

With this afore mentioned plan, the importance of homework and being super organised are important aspects to kick-start your exam year. In my opinion, homework is the best form of study and you need to be disciplined with it. Write homework diligently into your journal each day and complete each piece like you are doing an exam question. Organisation is really important during your final year, but remember it is an ongoing process. Every day, I make a list of tasks on my phone that I need to complete. At the end of the day, I review this list to see how many of them I actually fully completed. Tasks unfinished are then moved to another day so that each task is eventually dealt with. At times, a task is postponed, but always gets completed unless I eventually deem it unimportant. You could apply this philosophy to studying, ensuring that everything gets completed as soon as is possible in the most efficient manner.

That Moment

Think ahead into your future for a minute and ask yourself these questions: When you receive the Leaving Cert results envelope from your principal and your grades are all you want and more, how will you feel? What kind of a moment will that be when you unfold that sheet out   of its envelope and know in your heart how hard you have worked for each and every single grade written on that paper? Think how proud your parents, extended family and friends will be of you when you show them that small but momentous piece of paper. How amazing can one piece of paper be? Use these thoughts and feelings to motivate yourself to great heights this year.

I achieved a result in my last year in college that I knew would set me afloat. That day, I couldn't have scored more eminently. Let me tell you, it wasn't through ability; it was sheer hard work and long hours. It was a single focused to achieve, sometimes against the odds. With my piece of paper that day, I couldn't have reached higher than Liverpool winning the Champions league or Kilkenny winning the Liam McCarthy cup. It was my pinnacle-almost life changing. Everything is possible for you now, as this is your time. To get to where you want to be, you need to put a system in place and start taking steps to make your goals happen.

Many past students have tried multiple methods in an effort to improve their use of time. I feel that what has worked and indeed not worked for others is definitely worth noting. Chapter Nine will provide advice from students who have been through the Leaving Cert as well as a comprehensive survey of sixty sixth year students, their comments and how best they prepared. Studying must be done in a coordinated, organised way, not just reading, learning off and hoping. The following are my forty recommendations to help you study smarter. They are collated in no particular order, so put a star on your favourites, put them into practice and tell your friends.

My 'Top 40' Ways to Studying Smarter

1. **Assess your study area:** The first thing you need to do is assess your study area. Even if you think that your study area is perfect, read on, as you may be able to improve it. The ideal study space is somewhere where external distractions are kept to a minimum and has an organisation about it. The following are the conditions you need to put in place to ensure you have the best possible study area:

   ♣ Find a specific place that you can use for studying i. e. a quiet space.

   ♣ Dedicate this place specifically to studying. Don't use it for music, texting, social media, or anything non-study related.

   ♣ Make sure your study area has the following:

   - Good lighting: studying in poor lighting conditions contributes to poor concentration.

   - Ventilation: the air isn't too hot or cold.

   - Comfortable chair: one with good back support.

   - Tidy desk: Put your notes out one subject at a time. A cluttered desk is very distracting.

   - Study materials: Be organised with pens/paper, specialist equipment e.g. set squares, log tables and coloured pens.

How does your study area stack up against this tick list:

Twelve Point Study Area Checklist

♣ I have a specific set place for study ☐

♣ Other people often interrupt me when I study here ☐

♣ I often hear a TV/Radio when I study ☐

♣ The chair/table I use are uncomfortable for study ☐

♣ The lighting in my study area needs improving ☐

♣ My study place reminds me of things other than study ☐

♣ Temperature conditions in my study area aren't great for study ☐

♣ I keep my study area neat and tidy ☐

♣ I share my study area with others ☐

♣ I am easily distracted in my study area ☐

♣ I am unhappy with my place of study ☐

♣ There is another more suitable place of study I could use ☐

2. **Sort out a study routine:** You should plan to study at the same time each day, especially during the school week. On these days, I would recommend that you commence study thirty minutes after completing your homework. This will eventually become routine as your mind/ body adjusts. You may even find you are enjoying it after a while, like some athletes get addicted to the gym. Our body likes routine as it learns to anticipate events better and becomes more familiar with them. A study routine becomes particularly important as the school year finishes and you are at home preparing for kick-off.

3. **Organise your materials/notes**: Have all the materials you need to hand for studying. Having to search for materials will frustrate you and by the time you are ready to go, you've lost a half an hour and are in bad humour. Develop a system that works for you, so that you can find what you need when you need it. There is no excuse for not having your notes organised. A suggested system is to have a ring binder for each subject. In each binder, divide each topic for the subject using card dividers. Subsequently, put each subtopic into punched poly pockets between these card dividers. It is never too late to get yourself organised. It is never too late to start studying. Never.

4. **List out the topics for each subject:** For each subject, list out the topics that need to be studied in your final year. Show the list to your teacher to make sure you haven't excluded anything. You need to be realistic in not expecting to cover them all over a short period, it will take time. Make a second list of the subtopics inside each topic. The full listing for each subject should fit onto an A4 landscape sheet giving you a quick reference summary of a subject at a glance. Each time you complete and understand a subtopic, tick it off until eventually you can tick off the full topic. I always find that ticking off lists and seeing them shrink gives a great sense of satisfaction. With the workload that you have, any little victories like this will be very welcome here.

5. **Take regular breaks:** Yes, really! Taking short five-minute breaks every thirty minutes should keep you fresh and focused. Make sure that five minutes doesn't turn into an hour! Go for a short walk, call up a friend or have a snack and then come back to your work on time. Some studies have found that having a natter with friends can have a positive effect on memory and laughing increases serotonin (the body's chemical that makes you happy). It is important to leave your study area during your breaks to get a change of perspective and return with renewed energy for the next session. Longer breaks are earned after prolonged study stints.

Enjoyable breaks will allow you to become more efficient with your study blocks over time. Try and get involved in different things on your breaks to maintain freshness during study. Any kind of training or exercise is an excellent use of longer break times, as sport is one of the bedrocks of a healthy lifestyle. Physical activity has been shown to improve memory and retention of information. You shouldn't feel in any way guilty about taking breaks as part of your Lifestyle Timetable (which I will explain in detail in Chapter Two).

6. **Mirror exam hall challenges:** I would recommend during the days leading up to the first exam that you get up at eight-fifteen a.m., have your breakfast and complete a full past exam paper from nine-thirty to twelve similar to the time the real exam will actually be taking place. This prepares the mind, body and even the arm for the process of rising, eating, and focusing on the task ahead. This process will mirror the challenges you are about to face and is a great way to prepare for the exam hall. This is a little known and under used tip.

7. **Stay alert and interested:** When reading, it is a good idea to make notes or highlight key terms. I would be of the opinion that you should always learn with a pen at hand. I believe that just by reading a piece of text, you are not actively engaging with it. In my experience, you will remember more by summarising it or even just by making markings on the page. This method keeps the brain interested in what you are doing. Other learning methods you might consider for variety include watching a YouTube video, doing an online quiz, or drawing a diagram.

8. **Use clever ways to remember content:** You need to use your imagination when studying – this includes putting summaries and lists in your bedroom and parts of your house to help you remember them.

   Over my Educational career, I based a lot of my preparation around summarising notes. For you, set yourself a target to summarise a chapter onto one A4 page and then summarise this page into bullet points using post-its or flash cards. Options here include putting ordered flash cards somewhere visible or sticking post-it's to an A3/A4 page. You now have a shortened summary (written in a language you understand) of a topic, instead of fifteen pages of text in a textbook. It's so simple and it works.

   Summaries will save you time. If you have layer upon layer of notes with weeks to go, it will be too much information to trawl through and the great thing about them is. They are easier to carry around with you. It's important to continually shrink your notes into manageable bite-size summaries; otherwise stacks of paper will be mind blowing. Effective study is based on working smarter not harder.

9. **Be ruthless with your notes:** Many students go to Educational institutions after Christmas to boost their store of materials and, of course, their confidence. However, I have seen many students over the years become overwhelmed with too much material and they just end up getting swamped not knowing where to start. In subject areas you find difficult, reduce your material into manageable, thought provoking snippets.

   If you take notes in class, make sure to date and keep them in order for revision later. It's amazing what you will have forgotten from fifth year and you may even be shocked at how disorganized you were back then. It is important to keep a record of what topics you have done in class and how long your teacher has spent on them. Keeping a record of topics completed in subjects will ensure you are clear on what has been covered and what still needs to be reviewed. Being persistently consistent in relation to your notes is a big factor in doing well in exams.

10. **Set goals and keep records:** Setting goals will help you monitor your study and will give you something to work towards. If you under perform in a class test, set a mini goal for your next test to improve by a certain percentage. In your school journal, write down all your goals and check them off as you complete them - call it a 'Leaving Cert bucket list'. Ultimately, use long-term goals to motivate you to Ace the short-term ones. Long-term goals might include a points target in your Leaving Certificate, a possible trip to third level or scoring that rewarding job later.

    A goal will help you get where you want to be. Reviewing the success of your short term goals every two weeks will give you a sense of achievement. Research your goals online, thinking about what it would be like to achieve them. Goals provide challenges, direct behaviour, improve performance, increase motivation and improve self-confidence. They can be as small as understanding the theme of a short poem to as great as being the CEO of a company.

11. **Eat your frog:** We all put off things we dislike, like going to the dentist. Start by studying the subject or topic which isn't your favourite. Look at the subjects you are struggling with, and then consider the topics within these subjects that you need to tackle. Do not avoid something if you don't enjoy it, as it will eventually catch up with you. My least favourite subjects in school were Languages, so I always tackled them first every evening. I also got my parents to help and quiz me when I was learning vocabulary, which proved very useful later.

    Your friends will tell you all about their extensive study plans; but are they just studying what they enjoy or are good at? You should have a positive can do attitude in relation to your study, planning out how much you are going to do. You must sit down, plan it, and deliver the hours on your less favoured subjects no matter what anyone else is doing. There is no easy way unfortunately; the sooner you get started, the better. I can assure you of a great sense of contentment and achievement from eating that frog.

12. **Reward yourself:** Don't forget to 'have a life' as you prepare for your exams. Reward yourself after a long study session with a trip to the cinema or visit to your friends. Try your best to develop your own balance between work and play. Ultimately, reward yourself with breaks - taking a reasonable break after every good hour's work. There is nothing wrong with rewards like chocolate, ice-cream or a packet of gummy bears; as everyone who has done something constructive deserves a little thank you. The best reward you can give yourself on study days are breaks.

13. **Attend class and listen:** Make sure you attend school every day and be in class, paying attention and taking notes as best you can. It is worth remembering that your teachers have been through exams with hundreds of students before you, so they are well worth listening to, especially during the last four to six weeks of term time. They will give you a good insight into subject possibilities and advice for the exam paper. If I were a student, I would attend class until the very last day to get every ounce of knowledge out of my teachers. Even when official class time finishes, you can still get in touch with your teacher if you have questions.

14. **Live in the present:** Writer T.S. Elliot once said:

"Time past and time future are all contained in time present".

Don't be giving yourself a hard time about the lack of study done in 'time past'. Conversely, it is also not a good idea to be looking too far ahead into the future as it can cause anxiety and tension about your workload or what may or may not happen. Speculation and worry can be draining so try to control it as best you can. Always focus on the here and now, leave the past in the past. If Cinderella had gone back to get her shoe, she would never have met her Prince.

15. **Exam paper focus:** Are you familiar with the layout of each exam paper and its marking scheme? If not, you need to get checking. You can source all the past exam papers in the 'Examinations Material Archive' section of the http://www.examinations.ie website. If you don't have a set of exam papers for each subject, don't delay, get them today. A large part of your revision should be to assess and practice answering questions from past exam papers (under time pressure) on the topics you have covered in class. Remember also that each subject's exam paper   is different so you need to get familiar with each one. You need to find out the exact layout of each one of them. Is there a choice in sections? How many questions do you need to attempt in each section? Are there short/long questions or both? And, most importantly, how long can you plan to spend on each individual question? Again being super organised is the key.

Practising past papers is great for revision. It allows you to assess what you have learned, what you need to revisit and gives you a taste for the pressures of the exam 'environment'. The weekend is the best time to practice past papers as you have more flexibility then to create exam timing conditions. You should train as you play; if you get used to timing yourself and keeping an eye on the clock, it will come easier to you on the day. This is one of my ACE tips for scoring high.

After you have completed some questions to a reasonable standard, ask your teachers to mark and give you feedback on them so that you can obtain the maximum benefit from your work. Remember only test yourself on questions having studied that material from the course. The earlier you get practising exam questions, the better. Start by attempting easier questions, graduating up to more difficult ones, using your notes and textbook to help you. You will notice your confidence building as the months go on. During these trial sessions, be vigilant in answering the question you are being asked. You will need to meet certain criteria to get to a specific mark on an exam question. Past marking schemes, which are available to download will provide you with all the details you need on this.

On completion of an exam question, double check all your answers against a good solutions book. These are widely available in most subjects and will give you an insight into the style, wording, layout and standard required of an exam paper answer.

See my website and blog for more information:
http://www.acesolutionbooks.com.

16. **Stay connected**: It is important to keep up communication with your friends and family around exam time. Let them know how you are feeling especially if you are anxious about a particular subject. You will feel so much better about a problem if you 'chat' about it to someone. It can be easy to get cut off from the outside world when you are highly focused, so try not to let this happen. Balance is the optimal situation here.

17. **Use your family:** Using your family to help you learn is a useful tool that few utilise properly. Some of your siblings will have completed exams and may be able to pass on some good quality information or advice to you, so remind them to save their notes. Even if the content of their notes isn't suitable for your learning style, their methods and notes structure could give you some ideas on preparation of your own. If you are the oldest in the family, get your parents involved and tap into knowledge and practical advice they may have on subjects they enjoyed in school.

18. **Stick to your plan:** You need to view studying in sixth year as a fulltime job making sure you stick to the plan you set out for yourself. In my opinion, this involves not having a part time job, getting that Lifestyle Timetable (See Chapter Two) in place, attending all your classes, and doing homework to the best of your ability. If on 'no

school' days you decide on nine a.m. as the start time for study, get up before then, have breakfast, get ready and begin studying at that exact time. The students that do well are those who apply this self-disciplined approach and it guarantees that you are getting maximum efficiency out of your time. A high level of satisfaction will come when you get your exam results; knowing you gave it your all.

19. **Watch the mad nights out:** In sixth year in school, you should keep the big nights out to a minimum, especially after Christmas. If you are going out, try to organise Friday nights as at least then by Monday morning, you will be well rested and ready to focus again. Getting to bed at a reasonable time and getting plenty of sleep at the weekend will allow you to stick to your goals and plans.

20. **Surround yourself with positivity:** Surround yourself with positive people in sixth year. Without sounding harsh, sometimes you are better off without friends that constantly let you down. To quote Hans F. Hanson:

"People inspire you, or they drain you - pick them wisely"

Friends who are always in good form can really give you a lift. If your friends or boyfriend/girlfriend of the time isn't supportive of your work and isn't giving you room for study in your life, it may be a warning sign of where the relationship is going down the line. The opposite can also be true.

21. **Re-write your key notes:** This is a study method that has been tried and tested over the years. You should make notes during the day in class and when reading through your textbook at home later. In both cases, copy these notes neatly into a second notepad/copy. Doing this is a really good way of getting facts to 'stick' and will help you learn faster. Rewriting notes in your own words is a short cut to understanding material on your course; as writing something down forces one to think more about the subject matter, increasing retention of that information.

The key to doing well in exams is adaptability and being able to think critically about topics in the exam hall. If you can adjust to change, cope with the unseen poem or unusual Maths diagram, the examiner will view you as standing apart from the rest. Your key notes should reflect you viewing a topic from all angles; finding holes in it, praising it, picking out the key information from it, seeing where it links into other topics and most importantly evaluating its usefulness. An insightful set of key notes have delivered excellent grades for my students over the years.

22. **Test yourself:** We are never really sure we understand something until we are properly tested on it. Am I correct? You don't need to wait for class tests or mock exams to see how you are progressing in subjects; you can examine yourself at home. You should sit a full past exam paper at home under the time pressure of a real exam, splitting a paper into parts initially and building up eventually to a full exam. Towards the end of the year, ask your class teacher to give you some extra class tests or exam paper questions so that you can try them under these conditions.

During exam revision times, it can be difficult to find a friend or family member to quiz you, which is why you might need to do it yourself. Learn how to test yourself and do it in as many different ways that you can by setting questions, writing paragraphs, answering revision questions etc. Quizzes are a brilliant way of making sure that all the information you need for your exams has been completely covered. Ask your friend to write you a quiz. Your parents can help too by examining you on material you need to remember i.e. facts or bullet points. My own mother was extremely good at this; helping me improve in History, Geography and Irish.

23. **Create your own revision/flash cards:** Ongoing creation of revision cards in your subject will greatly enhance your learning. This type of revision is now very popular with students. Make revision posters, laminate them, and stick them in the shower, the bathroom, the kitchen; everywhere. When writing revision cards, split the card in two and write short phrases on one side and their explanation in your own words on the other. Colour code your quotes, dates, names, theories. Keep the colours consistent so that you will recognise them easily. Developing your own colour coding system will help you recall information quicker. Find out what works for you and constantly repeat the trick.

Every year, I see former leaving certs passing on notes to their friends. This has some obvious advantages, but there is no substitute for writing your own set of notes. Writing a summary of existing information switches your brain into content analysis mode and you will remember much more of the notes written by yourself compared to reading and trying to understand someone else's.

24. **Rotate your place of study:** It is good practice to rotate your study location, as if you start to get bored there, you'll associate boredom with learning. Try other places such as the kitchen table, the park, the library; anywhere you want to really. Try revising certain sub topics in unusual locations. An example of this could be to learn English drama quotes in your garden. When you need to remember these quotes in the exam hall, you can visualise yourself being back there, recalling the day you learned them and hopefully triggering your mind to remember them. Experiment to see if music or TV helps you concentrate. Some subjects will be more suited to this than others. I believe some Maths topics do not require one hundred percent attention but this may be associated with my aptitude for the subject?

25. **You are either studying or on social media:** Which? There is no problem with ventures onto social media any time during the year but I believe if you are inside a thirty-minute study block, stay off Facebook, Twitter, Instagram, Snapchat etc. al. I really feel you need to leave your phone elsewhere during these ultra-hard concentration sessions as nothing harms productivity as much as constant notifications from social media. As I have said previously, set your phone to silent or, even better, turn it off completely and only check social media during your set breaks. Being a screenager around exam time will distract you from your key short-term goals.

As for your computer, there are sites available that can block social media for a set amount of time, making it impossible to access until the time limit is up. This could be very helpful for you Facebook addicts out there. We've all been guilty of spending too much time on social media but there is a time and a place for everything. Try a blocking app that will temporarily keep you away from social media sites – there are plenty in your app store. If you are in an exam year, work out the amount of time you spend surfing on your phone/laptop every week. Can you afford to spend this amount of time on it from now on....? Think about it.

26. **Think outside the box:** If the usual studying methods are not working for you, you need to think outside the box. Try and come up with new ways to study. Use acronyms, create raps or songs to help aid memory. Associate your notes with lyrics from your favourite tunes. A good technique is to read your notes aloud and record them using your smartphone. Listening back to them will help you absorb the information and keep your memory sharp. Some students swear by listening   to lectures or audio notes at double speed! You can import audio files to free software like Audacity/Zamzar and then transfer them to your smartphone.

    I have used this method myself when I converted essays I was lecturing on into audio files. I then played them via my phone (using the AUX connection) in the car on the way to work. The advantage of this method is that you can educate yourself 'on the go'. Audio files are a good option now with all smartphones having the facility to record. Try by recording an English poem into your phone, constantly play it back to yourself, in order to get an insight into its theme. Various content from subjects can be recorded and replayed on your phone. You are only limited by your imagination.

27. **Stick your stickies**: I have known top students to have sticky notes stuck to the inside of cupboard doors, on the edge of mirrors, laptop monitors, TV screens, etc. Anywhere your eyes fall, you should put a post-it (sticky note) with key information on it! Repeatedly seeing information as you walk past or glance in the mirror will help to secure it into your long-term memory, in the same way that seeing adverts helps you remember a brand. Use different coloured and sized sticky notes for different subjects. Again, it is all about developing your own system and methods that you like.

28. **Would a study buddy/group suit?** If your class mates are keen on mass study sessions in the common room but you find them a waste of time, you may have to be a tad unsociable for a few weeks. Try to identify which environment you find most suitable to study in. Some people work better in a small group or with one other person, as they

really struggle to motivate themselves on their own. Asking your friends questions in a small group is a very effective study method, as long as you stick to the topic. We studied in groups for a small number of modules in university and found it useful in fact-based subjects, where we rattled off stats and opinions to each other that many of us remembered later.

Collaboration with one or two friends for some subjects is advisable, but not in large groups. In a large group, you end up with too much information that you haven't time to process and condense. Too many voices can lead to chaos and too many opinions can lead to a lack of conclusions. Collaboration is particularly good in fact-based subjects like History, Home Economics (S&S) and Biology as you can get a good flow of information going between you. It may not be as useful in Irish, Music and Maths as many topics in these subjects need to be worked on alone. Be decisive in relation to study adjustments you make, whether that be alone or with your study buddy. Sometimes it is difficult to measure the success of a study technique prior to testing, so make the decision and trial it. The road of life is paved with flat squirrels who couldn't make a decision.

With a trustworthy study buddy, you can divide work up, teach each other and share notes. Studying on your own for the last few months can get boring and tedious. Rotate your study between working alone and with your friend(s) – this will keep you fresh. Work to your strengths is the advice here.

29. **Use small (A5/A6) hardback notebooks:** Use a notebook for each subject to write down the keywords/phrases and vocabulary for each topic. This will help to improve your knowledge and understanding of a subject. The beauty of a small notebook is its portability. It can be carried around with you, adding variety to your learning. I always get my students to purchase a small hardback and prompt them to input important information into it every so often. By the end of the year, they have a pocket size set of notes great for revision. When studying your main notes, select the key words or phrases which will help you to remember what the topic is about, and then transfer them into your notebook. Your notebook will be a useful resource that you can dip in and out of as the exams approach and it won't seem as daunting as a big hardback!

30. **Become an active learner:** During study sessions, always have a pen and a highlighter to hand. You should mark the key points on your textbook, write brief comments at the side of the page or underline the important sentences. This information should be transferred to a summary page later. I really like this method of study as it reduces the quantity of notes and there shouldn't be a need to revisit that part of your textbook again. Active learning is a great way to keep yourself tuned into what you are studying.

31. **Rotate your learning:** The brain can only concentrate on a topic for a certain period of time. At times, when I was penning this book, I needed to get away and come back to it in order to maintain my focus. Rotate your work between memorising content, writing, oral work, audio, Internet research and watching documentaries. Most importantly, rotate your subjects. We all enjoy discovering about subjects we find interesting but it is so important not to forget the subjects you find difficult or the ones you are just not as interested in. Rotation of stimulus will trick the brain into performing better and going for longer.

32. **Be wise in your judgements:** Come the month of May, as regular as the clock ticks, the rumour mill kicks into action. "Oh, this is coming up this year", "I heard this is expected to come up", "There's no way that will be on the paper" are the kind of comments you can expect to hear in conversation both online and offline. Please be aware that if a topic is listed on the syllabus for your subject, it can appear on the paper even if it came up last year. Your teacher will source you a copy of the syllabus document if you wish to view it, or alternatively you can download it online. The syllabus document will tell you exactly what can be examined in the subject.

In relation to exam preparation, I know you all will try cutting corners; you will predict, throw topics away and ignore information. I would not recommend leaving out big chunks of the course. The SEC, who set the exam papers, state that they do not want any element of predictability in them, so in general my advice is to cover your bases well. However, consider this: You should continue to whittle down and reduce the volume of your keynotes. I am convinced that summarising information helps assimilate it better and leaves one with a more concise set of notes.

As exams approach, be careful who you listen to. Teachers with many years' experience (whether that's your subject teacher or someone you know well) won't put you far wrong. Having seen many exam papers, I think you can certainly place a good level of trust in them. The newspaper revision supplements, written by experienced professionals, can be a useful revision aid also.

33. **Time is of the essence:** Starting a study routine early in the year will boost your confidence and reduce any pre-exam stress by avoiding last minute cramming. Procrastinating (putting things off) is a common trait of all students. At a point during your sixth year, it will register with you that you have exams at the end of the year. I hope this point will arrive early in the year for you. A lot of preparation time is necessary prior to the Leaving Cert, but the real learning and understanding only follows during the last month or so. Every day is important and the closer you get to the exam the more vital these days become. Chapter Two goes into more detail on how to use your time more efficiently.

34. **Homework is study:** Homework done to a high standard is a brilliant form of study. Reviewing that days class via mini test questions or checking what's coming up tomorrow is part of your homework. Homework teaches you to analyse the information your teacher has given you. I always encourage my students to spend the first five minutes of their homework recapping what the teacher taught in class that day. Always take pride in the homework you produce, as it will stand to you in the end.

35. **Try mind maps:** A mind map is a diagram that organises information in a visual way. Many students prefer to learn visually as opposed to just reading text. I would recommend you create some simple mind maps in fact based subjects to help you remember material. On an A4 or A3 sheet, enter the core topic in the centre of the page with associated subtopics spiralling out in a spider like diagram. Putting mind maps on the wall at home will help you remember content and more importantly the linkages between topics and subtopics. If you are a visual learner (learn easily from pictures/diagrams), this technique is well worth investigating. There are lots of excellent

websites that will guide you through the creation of mind maps to enhance learning in many of your subjects.

36. **Know your keywords:** There is a set of keywords associated with each subject and knowing exactly what they mean is important in the context of gaining a successful Leaving Cert. You should learn at least two or three new words in each class every day and it is important to note them down somewhere. Your teacher will know the words that are more likely to appear on the exam papers, so you should listen out in class as they emphasise these during the year; they may even have a list of them explained somewhere that you can get a copy of. As a student, I would make a list of words and their definition for each subject. Your A5 notebook is an ideal place for these keywords. An example of keyword use is illustrated in Chapter Eight, where I list sample keywords/phrases and their explanations in Maths.

   Be aware that verbs mean different things in different subjects. For example, what does Solve, Evaluate, Differentiate mean in Maths? What does Describe, Find and Explain mean in Geography? What do Reflect, Discuss, Evaluate, Compare and Contrast mean in English? It is also worth noting that the same words can have a different meaning depending on the subject, for example "Evaluate" in English is different to "Evaluate" in Maths. When you are entering words into your notebook, it is important to explain the word in language you understand so that you can relate to it later.

37. **Linkages:** When preparing notes or indeed writing exam solutions, try and develop as many linkages between your subjects as you can. Any creative linkages look impressive when expressed on an exam paper. Linkages between subjects and indeed topics show your use of higher order thinking and indicate you have spent time contemplating what a topic is about. The advantage of having links to draw on is that you can use them in numerous subjects, in essence, two for the price of one. Mind maps mentioned above are a great vehicle for identifying and recalling linkages between subjects.

38. **Be positive:** Being positive will vastly improve your attitude towards study and therefore its quality. You should always focus on what you have studied, what you have learned or what you know as opposed to continually looking at what needs to be done. When you come

across an awkward question, you need to box it off properly in your mind. Instead of thinking, "we haven't covered this!", "how is this relevant to what I know?" or "is this even on the course?", you need to reflect on how it links into the material you have spent at least two years learning about, writing notes on, and listening to your teacher speak about.

The same goes for studying prior to the exam. Take control by changing the way you speak about your preparation. Instead of saying "I should be studying more"; be good to yourself and say, "Well I did a solid two hours this morning and will go back to it tonight". Change "I should be…" to "I'm going to…" Research has shown that positive language can lead to more positive results. If you say: "I can't climb that wall", you are less likely to succeed in the task, as your brain has almost been auto programmed to fail. This equation of positivity is worth noting at this point:

Positive attitude + Positive actions = Powerful results

39. **Pay attention to detail:** You will practice many past exam questions in preparation for your exams, so get used to paying attention to every single word to ensure you don't misread them. The mind has been known to play tricks when under stress, so be clear on what the instructions on the paper are. I always get my students to circle or underline keywords in past exam questions that we do together. Watch out for questions with two or three parts in them and also be careful how you write things down. Layout your paper well and use arrows and notes   to signpost the examiner around your answer book as required. Two acronyms that you should stick up on your wall at home are "Read the Full Question" (RTFQ) and "Answer the Full Question" (ATFQ). If you attend to this level of detail in class, Christmas and mock exams, it will be second nature come the Leaving Cert.

40. **Good days and bad days:** In preparation for your final exam, you are sure to have good days and bad. There will be days that you will not want to study, see notes, or maybe even go to school. It is how you deal with these feelings and situations that will be the key to your success in sixth year. You will learn lessons of perseverance during the year and will need to dig deep, draw on your energy reserves and

show determination also. Remember, energy comes from the five e's; exercise, endorphins, enthusiasm, exuberance and excellence. You will need to take ownership of your work for the first time ever. Try and stay positive during the bad days as things can turn around very quickly in life. When I look out sometimes at the rain pouring down from grey skies, it seems never ending; it does end though and sun can follow very quickly thereafter. If you don't feel like doing anything for a day or two, do so, but reset your goals to be back in top shape afterwards. Conversely, if you are having a great day and feeling good about the world, hit the books hard and go all out to maximise your notes and learning on that day. In general, be focused, determined, committed and persistent.

ACE Inspirational Quotes

———— ♥ ♠ ◆ ♣ ————

"Education is the most powerful weapon which you can use to change the world"
Nelson Mandela.

"I'm looking forward to influencing others in a positive way.
My message is you can do anything if you just put your mind to it"
Justin Bieber.

Chapter 2:

Your Time & the Lifestyle Timetable

Have you ever felt you'd like a few more hours in the day to study, play sport or even sleep? We all know this won't happen, so you need to maximise the time you have, well for your exam year anyway. Today, there are many demands on our time that we need to be ruthless, otherwise it will slip away. You need to be realistic with your time, for example, I am not going to set a reminder to complete a task at two p.m. on a Monday when I'm busy in school. I'll set it for a break time or after school when it is more likely to be done or at least assessed. The art of achieving optimum effort is selecting the best task to do, do it the best way you can and be effective at doing it. Some of the road blocks to being effective are:

♣ Interruptions slowing you down.

♣ Trying to be a perfectionist.

♣ Not using time during the day efficiently.

♣ Worrying about how much study your friends are doing.

♣ Just talking about what you are 'going' to do.

"You can't cross the sea merely by standing and staring at the water"

Rabindranath Tagore

Your Time

There have been stacks of books written about time management over the years. If you get your ducks in a row in relation to time management, you are more likely to deal out the perfect hand on exam day. When you were growing up, your parents told you where you were going and what time you were leaving etc. Now that you have more control over your time, you need to learn to manage it better, especially if you are studying for an exam. It is a good idea not only to think about your use of time but also to consider the following adages in relation to it:

- ♣ Time or Tide waits for no man (or woman).

- ♣ When God made time, he made plenty of it.

- ♣ To save time, you must spend time.

- ♣ Time is of the essence.

J.W Goethe once said:

"One has always enough time, if one applies it well".

As a student, I am sure your teachers have spoken to you in relation to having a balance between study, exercise, socialising, meeting your friends and relaxing. Your teachers are correct to refer to this balance. However, it is important, no matter what, to prioritise study during your final year in school. It must rise from the bottom of the list of your priorities to the top. The length of time you spend studying is not as important as how you study - quality over quantity. I would like you to approach studying as a journey, finding out new and interesting facts along the way. Vary your time with the many different ways that you can study, which I have discussed in Chapter One.

Get up, Dress up, Show up and Never Give up

In general, the most important thing you can do with your time in sixth year is attend school. Get up, dress up, show up and never give up. If you feel unwell in yourself on a given day, try everything you can to drag yourself into school. Obviously, if you need to rest or recover from illness, you will need to stay at home. However, I would advise you not to use every little excuse to avoid school. In my opinion, presence in school is more important than any use of your time at home. The more often you see your teachers, the more information and advice you will receive from them, the better quality notes you will have and the more up to date you will be with exam information for each subject.

As a teacher, I hear of many students getting part time jobs while in school and sometimes during exam year. This, in my opinion, is very poor use of your time. Do keep in mind that you can work in posts for the rest of your life and that there is only one Leaving Cert year. Call me a 'kill joy' or whatever but I don't think you can function well and study properly if you are working long hours over the weekend or during the week. You may get away with it in fifth year but not in third or sixth year. Why do I say this? Well I have seen many of my students try it over the years. They get a taste for 'going out money' and the books are fired in the corner or worse they are never taken out of the schoolbag!

If you are working at the weekend and feel it is affecting the quality of your study or if you are feeling tired in class, it may be worth parking the job until July. I am thinking of one of my students recently who was working a part time job up to five days before the exams. She was a very capable student in my subject, but ended up scraping the bare pass in it. I feel she underachieved as her mind wasn't one hundred percent on the exam. It is obviously your decision how you spend your time, but this is one thing I feel strongly about.

The Best Use of Time

In sixth year, I recommend that you target at least two hours homework and one-hour study each day during the school week (Monday to Friday), especially if you have put a good day's learning in. Further time spent studying may not involve constructive retention of information. If you have your work done for the following day's classes and find yourself falling asleep; stop, and go to bed. Your body is telling you to rest so it is advisable to listen to it. Revision and homework doesn't always have to be written, although if you are recalling something the teacher said that day, it is a good idea to write it down. Time spent on homework is always time well spent.

Many schools set up supervised study evenings for their students after school. If your parents can afford it, I would highly recommend you sign up, as it is a great opportunity to get your homework for the day done in a quiet learning environment. Supervised study will bed down regular study habits, as you have no choice in there but to concentrate and do work. You may also have the bonus of having a supervising teacher in there that you can ask questions of (nicely of course). If you have any energy left for an hour revising when you get home, use it.

The best use of time as the exams approach is to do questions against the clock. I believe it is crucial to practice past exam questions under exam conditions at this stage. You should put the clock on exam questions regularly and get used to the pressure of having to attempt them within the allocated time. With the question attempted, approach your teacher the next day asking them to have a quick look over it. If any of my students produce extra work, I am more than delighted to help.

Over the years, I have had the odd student who got caught for time in their exam. One of my former students, who was aiming high, just came up short of required points for his course. When I asked him what happened, his reply was one that every teacher dreads… "I ran out of time". You need to make sure you aren't that person who doesn't get the paper finished. Imagine having a large workload completed, knowing a swathe of material but getting the timing wrong. How frustrating would that be? If you run out of time for a question part, just move on, otherwise, there may be a part with more marks you may not even get to. I highly recommend you focus strongly on timing in your preparation.

In relation to the advised time of day for studying, get up early if that suits you. Personally, I study better late in the evening, but most prefer to work in the morning. As I have stated in the Preface, learning is about playing to your strengths, so study at the time of day your motivation is highest in order to maximise learning. Use the talents and gifts you have been given to study smart. This will create more space for the three f's: free time, friends and fun. Again, take all these factors into consideration when you are creating your Lifestyle Timetable (as detailed below).

Another good use of study time is to work with a study buddy. It is calming to have someone to talk with and bounce ideas off, but most importantly you won't need to spend as much time preparing notes, as the work can be divided evenly between you. This will free you up to concentrate on more important tasks. The "Learning Pyramid" theory adapted from Edgar Dale (Audio) states that students that teach each other retain ninety percent of content taught and fifty percent of what they discuss. If you compare this to the narrow end of the pyramid, research has shown that students retain only five percent of what they hear in a lecture (when your teacher gives information) and ten percent of what they read themselves. These statistics prove that collaboration and discussions with peers can be a great pathway to success.

Putting all the above into practice along with a structured timetable for study is a great starting point for success. This timetable is generally known as a "Study Timetable" but I believe you need to go one step further and create what I'm calling a "Lifestyle Timetable".

What is a 'Lifestyle Timetable'?

Every day you live by timetables; bus timetables, class timetables, gym timetables etc. I want you to think about what these timetables do? I am sure you would agree that they bring an order and certainty to your life. You understand that you have to be at a bus stop at a certain time to catch the bus or have the specific books to hand when the bell rings for class. There are plenty of apps, study templates, calendars and websites that claim they have the best study planners for you. Before you go downloading or signing up, I would get a pen and paper and sketch a proposed timetable for the next seven days.

If you create what I'm going to refer to as a "Lifestyle Timetable", you will become an expert at managing time. On a Lifestyle Timetable, you will enter other elements of your life outside your study and exam preparation in order to achieve a balance. Putting a "Lifestyle Timetable" together is the first step in taking control of real exam preparation and it will give you substantial inner confidence when you start implementing it. The idea behind it is to create a good lifestyle balance, your own subject rota and the flexibility to factor in unexpected events.

I view a good Lifestyle Timetable at the opposite end of the spectrum to last minute cramming, with the key being planning and flexibility. Whether it is for a short period of four weeks or a longer one of twelve, creating a weekly plan will help you manage your time more effectively and keep you motivated. The saying "Time and tide waits for no man" always reminds me of the future. Please keep in mind your exams will come whether you are ready or not. They don't care how prepared you are and will be timetabled (regardless).

Creating Your 'Lifestyle Timetable'

The following are the ten steps you need to put in place to get your first Lifestyle Timetable up and running:

1. **Create Blocks:** Draw out a large rectangle representing your week on an A4 sheet (landscape). Divide the week into thirty-minute blocks from nine a.m. in the morning until ten p.m. at night. Put a small five minute break block at the end of each thirty minute one. If it is a school week, you will be creating your Monday to Fridays study blocks from four p.m. until ten p.m.

2. **Commitments:** Write in all the things you have committed to for that week. These are fixed activities for that particular week that you must attend. For example: school, meal times, basketball practice, swimming lessons, attending church, etc. You won't have a massive amount of commitments in exam year compared to TY or fifth year and if you do, you may need to prioritise the important ones. Note that there could be a different set of commitments for each subsequent week's timetable.

3. **Prioritise:** List the seven or eight subjects you study in order of difficulty for you. In other words, list your subjects from one to seven, one being the most difficult and seven being the easiest in order of priority. Take into account how much you like the subject when ranking it.

4. **Breakdown:** Break down each subject by topic and sub topic on a separate A4 sheet, so that you can tick them off as they slot into your new timetable over the weeks and get completed. For example, a subtopic in history might be 'Renaissance artists'. Creating this summary involves a bit of work, but it will be well worth it, as it will give you a full subject overview at a glance.

5. **Frog Subjects:** Fill in your first set of sub topics onto your blank study blocks for the week. These are sub topics in the above-mentioned subjects you find the most difficult or those which are not your favourite (subjects ranked one to three). You should consider giving slightly more blocks to these subjects than the ones ranked four to seven (see point Six below). The distribution and balance of blocks will depend on your week and how you are feeling. Thirty minutes is enough time to spend studying a subtopic otherwise you will lose interest and motivation for it. By using this method, the subjects top of your priority list are never ignored i.e. 'Eat your Frog' from Chapter One.

6. **Fav Subjects:** Subsequently, enter the subjects you are good at or like, remembering you always need to leave some free wind-down time before bedtime. These subjects will be ranked four to seven on your priority list. The study blocks just before bed time should be topics you enjoy or work that requires less thought. It is great to end the day on a positive note and you will sleep soundly after finishing convincingly. Something pleasant you might enter into a late evening slot would be an English poem or some easy Maths, depending on where your best skills lie.

7. **Rotation:** See how you can build in rotation of learning styles into your study blocks to keep your brain interested. Rotate your study blocks between learning things off, listening to audio, creating mind maps, online videos, writing, doing summaries, creating flash cards, reading textbooks, drawing diagrams, discussions with your friends, Educational television/DVD, rewriting notes, reviewing class work etc.

See Chapter One for more information on studying smarter which links in with this.

8. **Breaks:** When you are entering your subject topics above, you will have a fair idea where you will need longer breaks. You have already set up your short breaks after each thirty minutes. It is recommended to take a longer break every two hours, using one (thirty minutes) or two blocks here. Along with breaks, include free time for leisure activities and meeting friends etc. Free time on the timetable will be determined by whether it is a school week or a week off school. Breaks, free time, leisure, and friend's time are all an extremely important part of whether the Lifestyle Timetable will be a successful one or not. Your Lifestyle Timetable will change every week and you will discover on completion of the first one, that successive ones will be so much easier to create and complete. In week two and three, you will be able to better judge your blocks and breaks and will move closer to a more realistic and better balanced timetable.

9. **Urgent or Important:** Your Lifestyle Timetable blocks for each week should reflect what is urgent and what is important for that particular week. It is important to be able to distinguish between "Important" and "Urgent" work. Homework will normally be urgent as your teacher will be requiring that within one or two days. Study itself is important unless it is within a month of the exams and then I believe it is urgent. Use this knowledge to work out how many study blocks you can fit into each week. For example, if it is a minimal homework week, you will have more room for study blocks and vice versa.

10. **Catch Up:** You should only plan a week in advance to ensure your focus is firmly on what's coming up. I would advise you to leave a few blank 'catch up' blocks at the weekend (when you have more flexibility), as sometimes things crop up during the week and you might lose the odd block. If you do miss a study block for whatever reason, enter that subtopic into one of these catch up blocks you've put in place. In this way, you never miss a block and eventually everything gets done. At this point, your timetable should now be full with a mixture of study, breaks, free time and catch up blocks on it.

From Christmas onwards, draw up this Lifestyle Timetable for each full week. Your lifestyle timetable will be different for a 'school' week than that of a 'free' week as school weeks will obviously involve 'school' and 'homework' time. It would be an idea to allow Saturday and Sunday to be interchangeable. In other words, if you have something important on Saturday, like a college open day for example, you can apply the timetable to Sunday and vice-versa. As you get closer to the exams, you may need to study on both of these days, but you can make that judgment for yourself.

The above are broad guidelines to help you put a lifestyle Timetable into action. You can alter it as required to suit yourself and once you have your own template that works, you just have to fill in the blocks each week. Try not to beat yourself up if things don't work perfectly, just get back in there on plan. The most important thing is to never give up; however, having a plan and being organised comes a very close second.

ACE Inspirational Quotes

"The harder I work, the luckier I get"
Samuel Goldwyn.

"I alone cannot change the world
but I can cast a stone
across the waters to create
many ripples"
Saint Mother Teresa.

Chapter 3:

Your Mocks

Within the first couple of weeks of your return after your Christmas holidays, teachers will begin speaking about exam papers, exam solutions, timetables, studying and more especially about the upcoming Mock/Pre-Leaving Cert examinations. These traditionally take place at the end of January or early February. If you are approaching these months, this chapter is a good one to read now. Many of my students get quite anxious about the mock exams as it is usually the first time they must sit down and do a full paper in the subject. However, as a Leaving Certificate student, you have all been through a similar process for the Junior Cycle and that should help greatly. Ultimately you should view the mocks as a reality check, a confidence booster, and an honest assessment. It is a way perhaps of taking stock of the work you have done and an assessment of what you still have to do. A few small but significant changes to the way you study will then pave the way to greater success. A quote from Robert Collier is apt here:

"Success is the sum of small efforts, repeated day in and day out".

It is normal to be nervous prior to the mocks, but remember it is an experience all exam students go through in Ireland, so try to enjoy it.

You will have endless questions in your head about the whole process before it starts. Questions like; has the quality of my study been good so far? How will I match up against my friends? What will my grades by like? Will I be able to manage my time properly for each paper? Am I doing the correct level? How am I supposed to complete an exam paper if we haven't finished the course? What will happen if I fail this subject in the mocks? Are the mocks harder than the actual exam? All these are normal questions to be contemplating.

The majority of schools run their mock examination timetable as a continuous block from start to finish and this will be quite a tiring and stressful stint for you. Some schools will have their mocks on the weeks either side of the mid-term which will give you a week's break in between. Other schools will run them the two weeks before mid-term and this will give some of you a well-deserved rest week after them. You have no control over the timing of your mocks, so the best thing to do is find out what's happening and start planning for it.

The Role of the Mocks

Firstly, your mock paper is created by one of several mock paper suppliers in the country. Each paper has been put together by subject teacher experts, external to the SEC. In other words, the body that will set your actual Leaving Cert paper has no connection or input into this one. The marking of the papers will either be done by an independent corrector or your class teacher, depending on school policy. The mocks are a trial run to achieve experience in sitting that subject, will test your response to stress and help you estimate the timing elements on a full paper. In general, they will give you an indication of where you are at; a snapshot at that moment in time.

It is important to note that the mock exams are quite different to the Leaving Cert, despite the fact that they are a dress rehearsal for them. Gaps between Leaving Cert papers will mean more time to study, rest, exercise, and eat properly whereas the mock exams will come one after another, day by day. Your teachers will probably use your mocks to motivate you and you can expect to hear them using phrases like "you have to do well in the mocks to stay at higher level" and other similar comments. The great thing about the mocks is that it will give you a fair idea if your approach to studying so far is working and what tweaks are required.

Prior to Your Mocks

To prepare for the mocks, I would create a Lifestyle Timetable (as per Chapter Two) the first week back after the Christmas holidays. In relation to getting ready for the mocks, try and keep a balance between diet, exercise, and sleep. Have a look at the structure of the exam and roughly the type of questions that might come up. It will only be around this time that you will be starting to get familiar with the expectations of the paper and you will learn so much from how the timing for each paper works out on the day.

Before sitting the paper, try to get somewhat familiar with the marking and structure of each paper. At this point you don't want to be planning to do two long questions in a section, when there are three to be done. When the mocks are over, you will start to look at these in a lot more detail. You need to be realistic about your mock exams, so try not to be putting any undue pressure on yourself at this point. All the real learning and hard work starts after the Mocks are completed, so again focus on the present and just do your best.

I would strongly recommend that you do not search out the mock paper you are about to sit, as this will distort your result. The idea here is that you want to gain a fair reflection of where you are with the subject at that moment. Also, it will confuse your teacher and parents in relation to progress, choosing levels and the amount of study you have done. Even though some students do it, it is a bad idea and will not stand to you in the long run. I advise you to make a genuine attempt at your mocks so you will discover your true strengths and weaknesses.

Mocks vs State Exams

As useful as the mocks are, it is important to understand that there are some fundamental differences between the mock and the state exams. Some of these are as follows:

- ♣ You more than likely have not covered the full course in your subjects, so you may not be able to attempt the full paper competently.

- ♣ You probably have had minimal exposure to past exam questions so you may not be fully familiar with the style, wording, and layout of the exam questions on the paper.

- ♣ You more than likely have never sat a full exam paper in this subject at this level before. You and your parents need to have realistic expectations about the mocks as a result.

♣ In general, the mock exam papers tend to be quite testing in relation to the actual standard of the leaving cert exam papers later.

♣ The mocks will serve as a motivator for you to work harder so that you can improve your knowledge going forward.

♣ The difference in the knowledge and vocabulary you will have at 'mock' and 'exam' time are poles apart.

♣ The mocks will show up your deficiencies and any gaps in your subject knowledge. Your experience and confidence will be so much better when the state exams arrive.

♣ You will have a much better understanding of the marking scheme on all your papers when the leaving cert arrives.

♣ Your mock results will be an incentive to put more work into your subjects especially if you are way off grade expectations. From this point of view, the mocks should be viewed as an opportunity.

♣ The timing of the mocks doesn't tend to be great for students as they can come very quickly after the Christmas break. Knuckle down, remembering you still have several months to improve grades in all your subjects and further familiarise yourself with the course.

♣ Think of the mocks as playing a league match in the winter as you prepare for the championship later in the summer. As Gaelic Athletic Association (GAA) folk will quickly tell you: *"It's the championship that matters"*.

Advice for Your Mock Exams

With your lack of experience in exam papers at this level, it is important to contemplate the following before sitting your mocks:

♣ Attend school for every single paper.

♣ Create a timing plan for each individual question and stick to it.

♣ Be realistic about your results as it is relatively early in the year.

♣ Eat well and get some exercise to give you plenty of energy for the exam hall and studying in the evening.

♣ Don't forget to have a look over the topics you covered in fifth year as they are now back on the table also.

♣ Have an idea what order you plan on doing the questions in – Start with a question you like or with something that is familiar to you.

♣ Keep the main focus of your study on the final goal, which is the Leaving Certificate. It is a marathon, not a sprint and the students that pace themselves well will do better.

♣ In preparation for your mocks, revise some sections of the course well instead of attempting to cover the whole course badly.

♣ It is OK to make errors in the mocks as you will have time later to learn best practice and use it. Making mistakes and forgetting things are all part of the mock process, so be sure not to be too hard on yourself.

♣ You don't have to be talented to do well in the mocks. We now know that hard work and studying smarter (See Chapter One and Two) is more important. Practice and repetition are key attributes to success for any student no matter how talented they are. It is true that hard work can beat talent if talent doesn't work hard enough.

♣ 'Control the Controllable's'. As you head into the mocks; get your energy levels up, have all your materials in place for each subject and ensure the house is stocked with good foods - these are the things you can control. You can also control how much study you do and how you react to setbacks; so much of the preparation is in your hands. As with any exam paper, you have no control over what is asked, so try not to worry about what 'might' come up.

Advantages of Doing the Mock Exams:

Many students feel that the mock exams are an inconvenience seeing them as two weeks study lost. Inevitably there are pros and cons to them, but for sure they will focus the mind for the months ahead. If during the mocks you find yourself demotivated, tired, anxious or disinterested, I can assure you that when leaving cert day comes, you will have greatly benefited from the experience. Here are some heartening reasons to persevere with the mocks:

♣ The mocks will serve as a walk-up call.

♣ The mocks will be an experience you will learn a great deal from.

♣ The mocks will motivate you to commence revision now.

♣ The mocks will help you identify topics you need to study.

♣ The mocks will test if your revision strategies are working.

♣ The mocks will familiarise you with the pressure of exams.

♣ The mocks will show you the areas you have good knowledge in.

♣ The mocks will gauge your performance against the clock.

♣ The mocks will allow you to practice exam techniques learned.

♣ The mocks will boost your confidence of success later.

♣ The mocks will show your teacher the areas you need help in.

♣ The mocks will get you familiar with the timing of a full paper.

♣ The mocks will give you an insight into the marking schemes.

♣ The mocks will increase your awareness of course content.

♣ The mocks will serve as an indicator to the quality of your study.

Mocks Will Guide Level Choice

Another big advantage of having sat through the mocks is it will help you decide what paper level you should choose for your Leaving Cert. Deciding levels is a tricky issue for students every year and involves many considerations. I would advise you to think about and discuss these factors in detail with your parents and teachers before attempting to change levels in any subject. Along with mock performance, here are some other considerations when making decisions regarding levels:

- ♣ Your teacher's opinion.

- ♣ Your attendance thus far.

- ♣ Your 'potential' points change.

- ♣ Your own gut feeling about the subject.

- ♣ How much you enjoy studying the subject.

- ♣ How much of the course you have done thus far.

- ♣ Results in previous Christmas and Summer tests.

- ♣ Results in class tests since the beginning of fifth year.

- ♣ The amount of effort you are putting into the subject balanced against the other subjects.

- ♣ Minimum course requirements for college (for example, do you I need a H7 in higher Maths to be accepted on one of my courses of choice).

Lessons Learned From Your Mocks

When your mock papers are assessed, the correctors will write some feedback on them. However, the best feedback you will get will be the experience of having sat down and attempted them. It is difficult to replicate that level of pressure at home, no matter how much you try. Consequently, you will be returned a bias free judgement on progress in that subject.

After you receive your exam paper back, complete the following actions in relation to your Mock experience:

1. Bring your exam paper to your teacher and ask them to give their view on where you can improve and pick up marks in the future.

2. Record the written and oral feedback from both the examiner and your teacher somewhere.

3. Act on this feedback to learn from your mistakes, so as not to repeat the same errors again later.

4. Have a think about what angle the questions were asked from.

5. Consider how well you did with timing on the paper.

6. Make a note of topics that came up which you hadn't covered in class.

7. Make a note of why you lost specific marks.

8. Make a note of anything that stands out for you from the marking scheme. Each teacher will have a copy of the said marking scheme, so feel free to ask them to have a quick look for more information.

9. Make a note of sections that you did really badly on. Add these to your upcoming revision list.

10. Make a note of what you did well, so that you can carry these positives into the future.

A small number of students get obsessed with their mock paper, trying to find out how to do every single thing on it and investigating all the places where they lost a small amount of marks. You must remember that some of the topics on the paper may not have been covered in class yet. I often see students' posting on the Internet, requesting different mock papers as the Leaving Cert nears. I believe you would be better served studying past exam papers from the department as opposed to trawling through unofficial pieces of work e.g. your mock paper. However, your subject teacher will advise you here, as mock papers in some subjects can contain useful resources.

So High the Climb, I Can't Turn Back now

Again, as in life, "you will learn more in the climb than by reaching the summit". The main difference between those who succeed in life and those who don't is the knowledge of how to get back up. If you do poorly in the mocks (which hopefully you won't), you still may be able to make a case to remain doing the same level. This will depend on your overall progress and study habits during the year. Being a hard worker is always your 'ACE' card in relation to any discussion with your teacher about level change. Sometimes it is easier to get lower marks on the higher level paper than well above average marks on an ordinary level paper and both results can yield similar points. However, only take on a certain level paper (whether that be higher, ordinary or foundation) if you feel confident about it or things can go horribly wrong. I'm thinking of a recent situation where I advised one of my students to drop down a level due to his results and ability. Unfortunately for both us, he didn't, and that particular exam didn't go well for him.

You need to consider potential point's totals when choosing your subjects, but more especially when choosing which level you are going to take each subject at. Have a look at the point's relationship table between higher and ordinary when deciding on which level to take. You must keep in mind that it is easier to drop from higher to ordinary, than moving in the opposite direction.

With the mocks done and dusted, you now need to turn your focus to the official past exam papers. Initially, I would firstly take a good look at the last four or five years and pin them down as best you can, completing as much of them against the clock. Upon completion of each question, I suggest you compare your work against a good quality solutions book. It is important not to give up too easily when attempting exam questions, considering that the complete solution may be found by approaching questions from different angles. As I will state many times in this publication, I feel that practising past exam papers is the best way to prepare for your Leaving Certificate. I have come to this understanding after years of preparing classes for exams.

In general, It is important not to over react to your mock results and it isn't helpful if your parents do so either. Your mock results will give you an approximate indication of where you are with subjects at that given moment, taking into account all the other information I have presented above. The key is not to get too up or down about them and just keep building on your knowledge, while maintaining focus on your final goal. You are in the process of catching and frying bigger fish, so just learn the lessons from it and move on.

ACE Inspirational Quotes

♥ ♠ ♦ ♣

"Start by doing what's necessary; then
do what's possible; and suddenly you
are doing the impossible"
St. Francis of Assisi.

"A mustard seed is the smallest of all seeds,
but when it has grown it is the biggest
shrub of all and becomes a tree so
that the birds of the air come
and shelter in its branches"
Gospel Acc. to Matthew Ch. 13 v24-43.

Chapter 4:

Stress Busting the Leaving Cert

Everyone feels stress from time to time. To me 'Stress' is a state of tension resulting from demanding or difficult circumstances. Stress is built into our systems to help protect us, keeps us alert and ensure we are ready to react quickly to danger. A little stress will push us to deal with life's challenges and can be good in small amounts. This is very much the case when it comes to exams, as our awareness of something important approaching is heightened. The key to dealing with stressful situations is getting to know your limits and learning how to avoid the triggers that stretch them.

The exam start date is now visible on your calendar and you are stuck indoors hitting the books while the sun is shining outside. With the weather improving and the calendar in focus, you can hear your teachers and parents speaking increasingly about the exams, as if you didn't know they were looming. Increased exam discussion may lead you to feel more anxious or pressurised. You need to have some strategies ready, to help you cope with feeling overwhelmed. This chapter contains plenty of ideas to relieve, avoid and deal with some of this stress.

Look After Yourself

If you tend to get quite anxious as exams approach, you need to know that this is normal, but at the same time, make sure and look after yourself and keep in touch with your friends. We as teachers know what you are going through during an exam year. We know how quickly orals follow mocks, how the media constantly writes about the points system, how your peers can unwittingly put pressure on you via social media, how your teachers pile on the homework and how project deadlines disturb the flow of your final exam preparation etc. It is important for you not to put extra pressure on yourself by keeping your expectations realistic. Your Leaving Cert year is only a short period in your life and it is important to look after your mental health and wellbeing before, during and after it. According to research from a national university, mental health issues among teenagers are three times worse than it was originally estimated several years ago; this is something new we all need to be conscious of. On the plus side, there are more conversations around mental health and more acceptance now that *it's OK not to feel OK* and OK to ask for help also. All of this is important during your exam year.

Nurturing your wellbeing by talking to people, discussing your fears and emotions, trusting people around you, keeping in touch with friends and overall being kind to yourself are key elements of maintaining good mental health around exams. Checking in with yourself in relation to these will serve you well as your career develops. If you find yourself getting overly worried or withdrawn from people, do not be afraid to ask for help, as you will feel much better when you do so. You are not alone in your struggles and the pressures you feel during this year will pass; the trick is to hang in there and try to think positively.

Change is one of the elements that causes stress in life. Examples of big changes include the death of a loved one, moving home, a car accident, or a relationship breakup. From my point of view, the opposite to change is consistency. To minimise stress around exam time, try to keep your routines the same as term time maintaining the same sleep, food, study, and leisure patterns.

Your body will thank you for it, as it won't have to make any major adjustments during this crucial period. If you feel yourself getting more worried than normal or your sleep is being interrupted as the exams approach, you need to make some little changes, as you are probably already 'under stress'. In the run up to exams, you need some practical steps and mechanisms you can call on to get you through. Have a look at the stress busting tips below that I promise will help. Subsequently, I will talk you through some simple techniques to deal with exam anxiety. Lastly, this chapter wraps up with some quick ideas for a calmer exam day.

Fifteen Stress Busting Tips for Exams

1. **Believe in you:** Way before you sit any exams, you need to instill some belief in yourself. You can start this process by making some simple changes, like the way you speak. For example: Instead of saying "I don't think I can do that", use language like "What do I have to do to achieve this?" Instead of "I'm not good at this", use "I can get good at this through practice" and instead of "I can't do that, it's too hard", use "What do I have to do to get better at this?" This positive can-do language reflects your potential to achieve great things. Positive Mind, Positive Vibes, Positive Life, Positive Results.

   In relation to your exams, you are well capable of getting what you want from each exam paper. You have studied each subject for many years and have every ability now to express this knowledge on the paper. After all those classes, without even realising it, you have learned so much from your teachers. I am pretty sure, at this stage, you have faced difficulties in your life and you got through them, didn't you? The most glorious sunrise comes after the deepest times of darkness. Millions have gone before you and succeeded, and now it is your turn to deliver and believe that you will. Never doubt yourself. Take each day of the exams as they come, focusing on the next upcoming exam.

   > *"Tired of trying to cram her sparkly star-shaped self into society's square holes, she chose to embrace her ridiculous awesomeness and shine like the supernova she is"*

   Unknown

2. **Take action:** If there is course material you are having difficulty with, getting stressed out won't help. Instead, I would encourage you to take action by seeing your teacher after class or even by asking class mates to help you understand the issues. Setting short term goals and acting on them is a great way of taking pressure off. Ticking off the most important items on a list and working your way downwards can work wonders. Always note down what you have done at the end of the day, not the

work you didn't complete. When taking action, make sure your goals are realistic. SMART Goals – Specific, Measurable, Action Oriented, Realistic, and Time bound goals can be achieved. Actions can be daily, weekly, or monthly. You need to write a shopping list of desirable achievements for each subject and get ticking.

3. **Keep in touch with friends:** Confiding in someone you trust, that listens and will be supportive of you is a great way of reducing stress and worry. Talking to a friend, relative or parent about study worries can greatly lighten the load. Often what seems like an overwhelming problem can be manageable when you talk it through with someone else. Your class mates are in the same boat as you and know how you are feeling; so you should help each other get through any issues. Support your friends and the sentiment is sure to be returned. Meeting up with friends who are not doing exams can also help to take your mind off things too. Stay positive, talk, express yourself and keep in touch with everyone.

4. **Don't be too hard on yourself:** It is important to understand that in any situation you can only do your best. The reality is that other students will perform better than you, but many will achieve lower results also. Not getting a top grade does not automatically mean failure and your parents and friends are there to support you with your efforts rather than your results. Try not to be too hard on yourself or compare yourself to your classmates. Ask yourself questions like... Why do I need this grade? Do I need this minimum grade to get into a course? Am I just putting unnecessary pressure on myself? Or am I doing this for my parents? Answering these questions will bring clarity to your motivation. Be kind to yourself during this stressful time, remembering that the Leaving Cert exam will not determine the rest of your life and most adults have changed career path two or three times on average. There are so many different avenues you can follow now, unlike previously, when there was only one direct route into a career. However, you do need an alternative post school plan to fall back on and this will help keep the stress levels down as the exams approach.

5. **Play is as important as study:** It is vital that you build in time to have fun and relax between study sessions. Use your Lifestyle Timetable discussed in Chapter Two to help you plan enjoyable activities of relaxation and

'play'. Going to watch your favourite team is a great way of taking your mind off exams. Listening to music works also, especially if you combine it with a walk. Neuroscientists have done research into the link between music and anxiety. They say they have discovered a song that reduces anxiety by sixty-five percent. The song is called 'Weightless' and is written by 'Marconi Union'. Download it.

"Life moves pretty fast, if you don't stop and look
around once in a while, you might just miss it"

Ferris Bueller

6. **Take breaks:** Breaks are to be viewed as a positive around exam time. Academics with high concentration levels know the importance of breaks. Air traffic controllers are forced to take regular breaks to ensure they stay fresh. If you find that you are losing concentration, take a short break – go for a walk, talk to a friend, or just do something different.

    When you resume study, you will feel refreshed and be better able to concentrate on your revision again. See Chapter Two for more information on the importance of breaks during a study regime.

7. **Liquid discipline:** I would discourage you from drinking too much coffee, tea, or fizzy drinks around exam time. Caffeine may key you up and cluster your thinking. Naturally you will feel a sugar rush from fizzies, but remember "what goes up must come down!" Just for this short period, maybe try some herbal teas like camomile or peppermint. I find peppermint tea is a great stomach settler.

8. **Eat healthy meals:** Eat healthily and regularly as best you can and do not skip meals around exam time, as your brain will benefit from the nutrients. Try to replace sweets and sugar with the so called 'superfoods' such as berries, bananas, oily fish, nuts and broccoli. 'Superfoods' can help boost concentration, energy, and mood. See Chapter Six for more information on eating healthy food.

"Eat your food as your medicines. Otherwise you
have to eat medicines as your food"

Amatellah

9. **Exercise the body as well as the mind:** Regular moderate exercise such as a brisk walk, a swim or session in the gym will boost energy, clear the mind, and help reduce feelings of anxiety. Exercise releases endorphins (the good mood feeling) and will help you see the positives of life. A walk outside will get air into your lungs with a short thirty minute stroll enough to reap many benefits. Seeing and breathing in the senses of nature has been proven to enhance relaxation. Team sports are also brilliant as they improve relationships with your friends allowing you to feel good about yourself. Sport will bring discipline to your studies as well as enhancing your personal confidence. From coaching Gaelic Football and Soccer teams over the years, I am of the opinion that the students who involved themselves in sport performed better in exams.

Exercise has been proven to have benefits as exams draw closer. The results of a University College Cork study (published in the US Journal of School Health) headed by Dr John Bradley, back up this claim. In the survey of over four hundred boys who graduated from secondary school between 2008 and 2011, those who participated in some kind of sports during the last two years of school "conferred an extra 25.4 points benefit to their final Leaving Certificate score". This increase is similar to what a student would receive from the current bonus point's structure. Need I say more? In other studies, it was also found that exercise helps one sleep better as the body is more physically tired (in a good way) and needs rest. In essence, when you exercise, your body produces endorphins which make you require more rest and feel sleepier.

10. **Do your best to retain control:** It is natural to feel some nerves prior to the commencement of exams, however getting excessively nervous is counterproductive, as it will hinder your ability to think clearly. Make sure to have a plan in place on the off chance that your mind goes blank. Remember, the best thing you can do is to try and stay calm and retain control of your emotions, as this will make it easier to recall information. Before the exams, write down all fears and worries in your journal. This will give you more of an awareness of what they are and why they are actually occurring. Writing things down also serves to ease the burden of carrying everything around in your head.

11. **Breathe deeply:** Slowing down and focusing on your breathing is a useful technique which lowers stress levels and promotes calmness. The quickest and most effective way to eliminating feelings of stress and panic is to close your eyes and take several long slow deep breaths, as breathing this way calms your whole nervous system. If you are breathing calmly and you still can't remember the information pertaining to a question, you should move on to another question and return to it later. Your teachers and/or parents will help you with some further calming/relaxation techniques if you ask them. Parents should encourage their child to practice deep breathing and use it as required both before and during their exams.

12. **Skip the post mortem:** Don't spend time holding a 'post mortem' into where completed exams may have gone wrong, as often we are our own harshest critics. You are better off to compete against yourself in exams rather than against your peers, as often competing against others can be unrealistic. After the exam, you should congratulate yourself for the answers you completed confidently, learn from the bits where you feel you could have performed better and move on.

13. **You can't control everything:** Always remember that you are not alone in your exam pressures and that there are over fifty thousand others sitting the Leaving Certificate with you. Talk to fellow students if you feel anxious, as this will allow you to air your views, and let's face it, having a rant every so often is no harm. As the exams approach, nerves can be turned into a positive, as they will help you focus on the task at hand. Making a list of your main concerns, circling the ones you can control. This will help you to realise that there are existing issues of concern that you have no control over and that sometimes you just have to do your best and accept things. It is always a good idea to focus on the worries that you have control over, as those are the ones you can positively influence.

14. **Drink plenty of water:** Hydrating yourself well by drinking a few glasses of water every day is really important as will be discussed in Chapter Six. Maintaining hydration levels will help you improve your performance from the start of the exams to the end. You cannot afford to be dehydrated as the exams approach, remembering that hydration is something that is built up in the body over a period of time. As far as I can recall, all the Leaving Cert exam students I

superintended this year had a bottle of water on their desk; they knew the importance of hydration.

15. **Have a Plan B for third level:** You need to be realistic with your third level course choices and obviously choose them in the order you wish to do them in. One thing I did notice this year was some students banking on one choice. I feel strongly that you must have a plan B in place, in case your first choice doesn't work out. Shooting for the stars is important, but you need to be aware that you could be unlucky and circumstances can conspire against you on the day. Have a look at every possible third level course and college and pick something that would interest you for your second and third choice. These can be used as a stepping stone to get back to your first choice later. Having a plan B is the ultimate stress busting tip as when you do your best and things don't work perfectly, there will be something there to catch your fall after all your hard work.

Techniques to Help Those of You That Get Anxious

If the thoughts of sitting exams fill you with dread, the more aids you have to draw on, the better chance you will settle and remain calm in the exam hall. The following are five anti-anxiety techniques that will help you maintain your zen on the day. Try them!!!

1. **Visualise what you need to do**: Visualisation is a technique often used to reduce anxiety. In this context, a few days prior to the exam, close your eyes and imagine yourself sitting in the exam hall. You need to picture yourself going into the hall feeling calm and confident in your ability. Imagine sitting down to read the paper and your mind going into a highly focused state and completing the paper full of confidence with many of the topics that you have prepared appearing on it. Imagine putting your points across on your answer book in a clear manner and being really content with your efforts made at the end. In general, you are visualising yourself doing well on an exam paper you are concerned about. You should reapply this technique then just before you actually enter the exam hall.

   This technique utilises and links with positive thinking. If you go into a football game, for example, thinking you will at best draw with your opponent, the majority of the time a draw will be the best result you will achieve. In other words, you have almost convinced yourself that you will not win this game. If you imagine you are going to do well in anything, you have a much better chance of succeeding in it. I am a firm believer in this type of positivity which ties in with visualisation. Henry Ford once said:

"Whether you think you can, or you think you can't—you're right"

2. **Try Neuro-Linguistic Programming (NLP):** Despite the complicated looking title, NLP can be broken into some easy to complete steps. I have tried this technique myself to reduce anxiety about something and it brought me back to a place where I felt full of confidence, belief and reduced my anxiety levels. To try this, close your eyes and take yourself back to a specific situation in your life where you were extremely happy, almost on top of the world. Every person will have their own unique situation. It could be something major you achieved in life, something big that you won or something amazing someone said to you to make you feel great.

   Think about the moment in detail, how good you felt during it, the surroundings that day, the background, the smells, the feelings, and the emotions that went with it. While doing this, take in big breaths, and release them slowly. While keeping your eyes closed, press your thumb against your index finger (the finger next to the thumb) retaining the feelings and thoughts from your happy place. Practice doing this a few times before exam day arrives. The next time you feel yourself becoming anxious or if you are worried on the day of an exam, try it. It should bring back those warm feelings of confidence and calmness to help you deal out that winning hand that you know you have.

3. **There's an app for that:** As you know all too well, there are apps for everything now. Do a search for the words "calm", "anxiety" or "stress" on your app store and download two or three apps to see if they would be helpful in calming you before an exam. You may even stumble across other useful Educational apps for your subjects, as there are loads of free ones available out there for foreign languages and subjects like Maths and History.

4. **Chat with your friends:** A parent contacted me recently concerned about their child locking themselves away from the world with the sole focus of studying. Is this you? It is important that you keep in touch with friends around exam time and talking through issues and problems based around the exams is one of the best forms of therapy. If I am trying to sort out a problem in my head, catching up with friends socially and explaining what's going on usually helps me simplify it. Almost immediately, I feel the issues around the problem become clearer upon speaking to someone about it. You know yourself that a fake reality can be created and grow in one's mind, so try and keep as much of it out in the open as you can, in order to keep your anxiety levels balanced. Conversations in person are much more beneficial than living in a sometimes false online world.

5. **Train yourself to think ahead:** Under stress, the brain releases a chemical called cortisol which raises the heart rate and clouds rational and logical thinking. We are all familiar with the "post mortem", looking back and assessing a situation to see how we can do things better in the future. An emerging idea is that of a "pre mortem". The way this works is to write down all the things that can go wrong and then you try to figure out what you can do to try to prevent them happening or minimising the damage from them. For exams, you need to think ahead to the potential pitfalls that could occur on the day in order to be better mentally prepared. The reality of any exam paper is there will be issues and surprises on it, in that it's almost impossible to predict it exactly.

I suggest learning a few actions to minimise stress linked closely to this idea of a pre mortem. Firstly, place any school materials you seem to easily misplace in a specific area at home. Any school stuff that lives at home should have this place of residence. The idea here being that if you lose something important, this will be the first place you will check for it. Secondly, I would have a plan B in place for each exam paper in case things don't work out as planned. If an unexpected scenario arises, hopefully it will be something you have considered as a possibility beforehand and therefore will be much better able to cope with it. This calmness will minimise stress levels and you will make better decisions as a result.

Simple Ways to Stay Chilled Around Exam Time

♣ Do things you enjoy on your breaks.

♣ Take regular exercise and meals.

♣ Reduce tea and coffee from the afternoon onwards.

♣ Work consistently doing something every day.

♣ Stop studying an hour before sleep time.

♣ If you are worried about something - write it down.

♣ Meet up and have a laugh with your friends.

♣ Create play lists of your favourite songs.

♣ Go for walks and cycles with your friends.

♣ Treat yourself to munchies every so often.

♣ Have a hot bath.

♣ Buy a colouring book.

♣ Prepare for the morning the night before.

♣ Don't rely on your memory, write it down.

♣ Say "No" more often.

♣ Avoid negative people.

♣ Always make copies/backups of important documents.

♣ Smile.

♣ Pet a friendly dog/cat.

♣ Pay someone a compliment or praise people more.

♣ Believe in yourself.

♣ Visualise yourself being successful.

♣ Develop your sense of humour.

♣ Read a poem.

♣ Learn to breathe slowly.

♣ Do it today.

♣ Work at being cheerful and optimistic.

♣ Do everything in moderation.

♣ Strive for excellence not perfection.

♣ Do something that challenges you every day.

♣ Feed the birds.

♣ Stretch and exercise somewhat every day.

♣ Always have a 'Plan B'.

♣ Memorise or tell someone a joke.

♣ Become a better listener.

♣ Get to school earlier.

♣ Clean out your bedroom.

♣ Plan ahead.

♣ Watch a movie and eat popcorn.

♣ Write a written letter to a faraway friend.

♣ Go to a match and scream your head off.

♣ Recognise the importance of unconditional love.

♣ Keep a diary.

♣ Get enough sleep.

♣ Do something nice for someone as often as you can.

♣ Thank someone for something they have done for you.

Your last year will go by so quick, so use every day in sixth year as constructively as you can. Despite it being an exam year, there will be fun with various school functions and nights out. There more than likely will be a 'final this and that', a graduation committee and ceremony, a debutant committee, a prize giving ceremony and a yearbook to be created as well as goodbyes to be said etc. These will occupy your mind and become welcome distractions during a tough last term. Some of the best fun I have had was in the run up to my Leaving Cert and College exams as tension was released through a strange kind of madness. It is important to be good to yourself as the year draws to a close, so try to enjoy every moment.

ACE Inspirational Quotes

"It's always darkest before the dawn"
Florence and the Machine.

"When you focus on your problems,
more problems occur.
When you focus on the possibilities,
you will have more opportunities"
Unknown.

Chapter 5:

The Best Leaving Cert Hacks

As a sixth year student, I realise that it's in your nature to look for shortcuts to try to improve your exam performance. Your teachers have covered a large body of work with you over the last few years and clever students will realise that not every single little thing is required to be known in-depth. It is only human nature to look for better ways to perform tasks that save you time, energy and stress. I am not advocating slicing off parts of the course but you do need to work smart. In this chapter I will provide you with some useful hacks to help you prepare more efficiently, focus better, study smarter, learn sharper and ultimately achieve more. This chapter contains practical solutions to real problems you may face as you get ready for exams. The following are:

My Twenty Definitive Leaving Cert Hacks:

1. **Subject choice:** At the start of fifth year, you have a big decision to make in relation to what subjects you are going to sit for your Leaving Certificate. You need to select subjects carefully as this will have a big influence on your points total and options later. If you are interested in or like a particular subject, you will be more inclined to want to study nd know more about it. I would strongly advise you to select subjects you enjoy, not ones that your friends are doing. On the other side of the same coin, I would say that if a potential subject is linked to a specific career you are considering and this subject is one you didn't enjoy for Junior Cycle, you should reconsider selecting this subject and possibly even your future career. If there is a specific course you wish to pursue, you need to check if there is a minimum requirement for a subject on it. It is true that second level subject choice has a big influence on what you go on to do at third level.

2. **Sleep consistency:** Sleep is an important feature of functioning well as a human being. We spend approximately thirty percent of our day asleep. Even more significant is that sleep from the night before affects how productive you are the next day. A lack of sleep can leave you feeling tired

or groggy and can affect your food choices the next day. Researchers from Ghent and KU Leuven Universities in Belgium recently surveyed six hundred and twenty-one first year university students about their sleep habits during exam periods. The findings showed that students who slept at least seven hours each night during the exam period did nearly ten percent better than students who got less sleep. I always feel that staying up late tends to link in with caffeine intake (which includes energy drinks) and altered eating habits. In the case of constant late nights, your body can struggle to re-adjust to a new sleep pattern.

As the last eight weeks approach, many sixth years get quite tired due to notes being fired at them from all angles in their subjects. The trick is to go to bed at the same time and get up at the same time every day, even on weekends. Are you tempted to stay up late on Friday and Saturdays? Is going to bed on Sunday a disaster as you struggle to get to sleep for ages? For the eight weeks prior to the exams, get yourself into good habits in an attempt to keep your body clock as regular as possible. Eight to ten hours is the recommended amount of sleep for a teenager so this should be your goal, especially around exam time. I would recommend aiming to be in bed by eleven p.m. and avoid technology including TV, mobile phones, and tablets in the bedroom after that. Remember, there is a small percentage of the population who can function perfectly well on four hours sleep a night. By the law of averages, you are probably not in this group.

In relation to your bedroom environment, I think it is important to leave your phone outside the bedroom or even better, switched off. Probably not music to your ears, but I am sure you will be grateful of the advice later. Our phones are not good bedtime companions, as studies tell us that exposure to the white light emitted by them affects our ability to reach a deeper sleep. This deep sleep ensures we wake well rested and fresh. Have you ever woken up exhausted and said to yourself "I shouldn't have stayed on my phone so long"? If this is you, well, you know what to do.

Similarly, many people use the alarm on their phone to wake them. I suggest investing in a regular alarm clock. There are clocks on the market now that will wake you gently with a gradual brightening light. Either way, the ideal situation is to leave your phone/iPod/tablet in another room. If you are struggling to achieve this, ask your parents to help you make this change. Using an alarm that doesn't set the room on fire helps one to wake up easier also. I find that setting a light alarm to go off first and a second more forceful one five minutes later works well for me.

The night before a big exam, the best thing to do is just stick with your regular revision routine and go to bed at a decent time, facilitating at least seven hours of sleep. A consistent temperature of around eighteen degrees is conducive to good sleep. However, you shouldn't change a winning routine and if you are sleeping well, I wouldn't advise altering it as the exams approach. Personally, I find a dark room with blacked out curtains allow me to sleep better, but again go with whatever your happy with.

As you get closer to exam day, you should have most of the hard work done, so trawling through large volumes of material late at night is pointless. Make sure you have all your bases covered so you feel confident, satisfied, and relaxed going to sleep. The idea of an 'all-nighter' is a disaster, as by two or three p.m. the next day, your body will start to switch off and your concentration levels will seriously dip. Exam times are stressful, therefore good quality sleep during this time is very important. Anxiety can seriously affect your sleep and conversely if you don't get a good night's sleep, you may get anxious. Loads of coffee or energy drinks to keep yourself awake the night before the exam is a no no, regardless of how tempted you are to do so. Drink plenty of water instead to stay hydrated.

3. **Avoid avoiding:** It is very easy to sit down after dinner in the evenings and start into the subjects you like. I would advise you to take on the subject you find most difficult or the one that is your least favourite first. When completed, this will give you a positive feeling as you tick it off on your timetable. You should then move on to your second least favourite subject etc. This links directly to the plan I have set out in Chapter Two to give less favoured subjects more blocks on your Lifestyle Timetable. In this way, the night's work is getting easier as your freshness wanes. Treat each piece of homework as a mini-study session and try not to rush it. Do whatever type of learning you don't particularly like first. In other words, if you don't enjoy reading or learning off, maybe do that first as opposed to writing or note taking. Homework and studying are all about tactics, planning and working smart; quality over quantity.

4. **Have realistic expectations:** 'This morning I'm going to go back through the biology past papers and do every question on reproduction' is your plan. A more intelligent approach would be: 'I will find one long exam question on reproduction, have a go at it and if I don't know something, I will look it up in my notes. I will then record the information I have learned into a little notebook for this topic, which I can refer back to later'. Setting expectations too high can foster negative feelings if they are not met. Remember, that the majority of actions in our daily life don't work out perfectly and sometimes you just have to make the best lemonade out of the lemons you've been given. Our brain is pre-disposed to cling to negative feelings and beating yourself up about not studying or not doing enough can become habitual. Darkness cannot be directly removed, but it automatically disappears when you turn on the light. Try to be positive by abandoning phrases like "I should have" or "I wish I had". Remember, you cannot change the past, but you can shape the future.

On following your Lifestyle Timetable over the next number of weeks, always keep in mind that you are only after small steady gains. Rome wasn't built in a day, so start somewhere and lay down progress, brick by brick, session by session. These will compound themselves over time into great achievements. To quote a famous Vlogger:

"When I embarked on making my first YouTube video for my website,
I had no idea how to do it. I decided I would just get one out,
knowing that the next one produced would be better.
If I had tried to make a movie trailer, the chances are there wouldn't
be any of my videos at all online today".

I have seen some of my students studying extremely hard for the mocks with their eyes hanging out of their heads by mid-term, and then they don't rest at all during their week off preparing for orals etc. Be realistic about what you can get done and always listen to your body. By all means go for it if you feel full of energy and enthusiasm but stop, rest, or take a break if you are feeling jaded, as it is a marathon you are on. If you start preparation early enough in the exam year, you will have loads of time to get there. As stated earlier, any good Lifestyle Timetable builds a good dollop of realism into it.

5. **Implement a weekly lifestyle timetable:** It is more important to have a plan and deviate from it than have no plan at all. A plan gives you a sense of control and with that comes motivation, which breeds confidence, success, and even more confidence. The Lifestyle Timetable detailed in Chapter Two is a straight forward plan to implement, so do it now. A clear plan allows you to have the visibility to see what is completed and what is left to be done; it keeps you honest. The only person you can't lie to or be brutally honest with is yourself. Deep down you know how much progress you are making and sometimes if things go wrong, you can put 'Plan B' into action to make amends.

    If you miss a study block, transfer it into the next available slot on the timetable; being honest with yourself is important, so be organised and make a note of blocks lost in case you forget. It's about being determined but flexible and doing your best of course. If your friend calls you to go out for an hour on Friday night, re-jig Saturday's timetable to get that hour back. The good students always find a way. Simples!

6. **The benefits of exercise:** Exercise is very beneficial in your exam year but it also sets in motion great habits for your future, making you stronger both in mind and body. I have discovered many positive benefits of taking regular exercise. Firstly, after exercise, I feel like I have pushed myself and done something worthwhile. Like studying, exercise is so easy to avoid; sitting on the couch telling myself that 'I will start tomorrow' always seems like the easy option, and maybe you feel like that with the books now. On completion of every mini session, I feel a great sense of achievement and the nice thing about exercise is that you can listen to your favourite music or bring along a friend for a chat also. I have more energy and my thought process is clearer after I take in fresh air. Being outside gives me time to think my way through the issues of the day and even come up with some solutions.

    I have also discovered my body accepts and digests foods more efficiently after exercise. They say a healthy gut is a healthy body and I always find an improvement in my digestion on the days I exercise. Lastly and most importantly, I feel more upbeat, productive, and just mentally that bit stronger after making the effort to exercise. I hope you will feel similar benefits by increasing activity or continuing what you already do. Some of you will reap bigger rewards than others, but I think there is 'one for everybody in the audience' here.

7. **Stay in the moment:** American poet and philosopher Henry David Thoreau once said:

> *"You must live in the present, launch yourself on every*
> *wave, find the eternity in each moment".*

Increasing awareness of the moment you are currently in, given the amount of distractions these days, is really important. I really like the phrase "the future is now" and being aware and relaxed in the moment will reduce exam anxiety. Our generation is constantly searching for something extra in life, looking to the future for the next buzz. I believe we need to live and enjoy more the moments we are in to be fulfilled.

As a student, staying in the present will greatly influence the quality   of your study. You can only control what you are going to do in your next study block and your focus needs to be on those notes in front on you now. Similarly, being aware of moments in the exam hall is ultra-important, as you cannot afford to let time pass you by in there. Have belief in yourself, that the hard work you have engaged in over the last few years is about to reap rewards. Be aware of exactly where you are and don't daydream or drift to the future. In general, worrying unnecessarily about problems and issues that may not even occur can waste a lot of energy; energy required both at your study area and in the exam hall.

> *"Worry is like a rocking chair; it gives you*
> *something to do but never gets you anywhere"*
>
> Erma Bombeck

8. **Pile your notes:** During my own exams, I used to pile summarised notes in my study area, subject by subject, topic by topic. Like the monkeys, I am still 'a believer' in topic summaries as detailed in Chapter One. As a teacher now, I still pile notes neatly for my classes. From a study point of view, it gives structure, separates one topic

from another and it allows one to find notes quicker for the next study slot. Afterwards replace the pile back into its subject section. If you are summarising and rewriting your notes properly, your subject piles should get smaller as the year develops. The best thing about note piles is that when you have completed the exam in that subject, you can put the pile away.

Gradually, the holes will start to appear on the floor as you complete subjects. This will give you a feeling of real progress being made.

9. **Be positive:** You should always try to have a positive attitude around studies, feeling content with your achievements. It isn't a great idea to spend time with people who have a negative outlook around exam time. You should always think about good grades and not consider negative outcomes. Many students are quite negative with talk of just "passing". I have actually banned the "F" word in my class totally; Fail. Something more amazing like a solid "H" or a high "O" is available to you, no matter what your level of ability is. Your abilities are the limits of your goals and imagination. A great exam student needs more than just ability; they need to apply themselves well to learning and working hard, so be heartened by the fact that you don't need to be academically top of the class to reach the top. It must be remembered that weak students can do very well in exams and highly intelligent ones can do badly. This should fill you with positivity to know that everyone is on the same playing field. If you are losing heart in a subject, I would refer you to the Leaving Certificate statistics online to consider how other students have performed over the years. You will be surprised how high the success rates have been.

10. **Try some memory techniques:** Memory techniques are a much under-utilised way of helping you recall important information. In my experience, they are your secret weapon on exam day. Here are four possible techniques to aid memory that you can use without too much effort:

>   **a) Chunking:** An average person can hold seven items (a chunk) in their short term memory. A chunk can be further broken down into seven topics with seven subtopics written as bullet points. This list in itself would almost constitute a full course

summary which you could transfer on to an A4 sheet, mind map or flash cards. You can break other elements of recall into chunks too – for example, most people break a phone number into three chunks (087) ----- 507 ----- 7655. If you are learning off a list, for example, seven characteristics of an organism in Biology, the most efficient way is to learn three off first, then the other four and finally put them together.

b) Creating an association: Creating an association between a topic and an experience in life will help you remember it better. Associations can be helpful to learn information like a new verb, formula, or rule. In the exam, you should call to mind the association to help you recall the actual information you need to answer the question on the paper. The following are some practical applications of using associations:

♣ Drawing on your own life experiences and applying it to a question on the paper.

♣ Creating mental hooks for a set of specific facts.

♣ Sticking a list of keynotes/quotes for an English play on your bedroom wall (use an A4 sheet so it is easy to read).

♣ Sitting out in your garden for thirty minutes to learn a specific subtopic.

♣ Brushing your teeth when recalling a specific list.

Another association method worth trying is to draw a skeleton to represent a topic, for example, the characteristics of a region in Geography. Label the main characteristics of the region onto the big bones (like branches of a tree) i.e. the physical, social, and demographical characteristics of that region. Write the finer detail then onto the smaller bones. The association of a skeleton on your wall will stick in your memory and help you to recall where the information is located on it and links between topics.

c) Repetition: As the name suggests, this is probably the best and the oldest form of learning. Sixty-six percent of material learned is forgotten in seven days and eighty-eight percent of it is lost within six weeks. These statistics highlight the need for repetition to enhance retention. Doing daily and weekly reviews by repeating the same learning patterns will help information stick. Repeatedly reading information out loud is a method used successfully by many students.

d) Mnemonics: Mnemonics is defined as a play on words, letters and rhymes to aid memory. This method of retention is useful for factual subjects like History, Geography, and Science. It involves the use of acronyms to recall bulleted lists. The great thing about Mnemonics is that you can create your own examples or search the Internet for more interesting samples, in whatever subjects you need them. This learning style is a good one to collaborate with your friends on. For example, set your two study buddies the challenge of coming up with five examples for a subtopic and later come together and share all fifteen with each other. It is advisable to write down all the acronyms you may need at the commencement of a given exam, so that you won't have to remember them under pressure later. In other words, scribble down what you know when you get in there.

Some examples of the use of Mnemonics are as follows:

♣ To learn the colours of the Rainbow, remember **R**ichard **of Y**ork **G**ave **B**attle **in V**ain (The first letter of each word represents the first letter in each word of the colours i.e. **R**=**R**ichard=**R**ed etc.)

- **R**ed, **O**range, **Y**ellow, **G**reen, **B**lue, **I**ndigo and **V**iolet

♣ To memorise the relationship between **D**istance, **S**peed, and **T**ime:

- **D**ads **S**illy **T**riangle: **S = D/T**

♣ To learn the Sin, Cos and Tan Maths formula:

- **O**h **H**ell, **A**nother **H**our **O**f **A**lgebra:

- Sin = **O/H**, Cos = **A/H**, Tan = **O/A**

♣ To memorise the Seven Characteristics of Living Organisms; **Mr Grief**:

- **M**ovement, **R**eproduction, **G**rowth, **R**espiration, **I**rritability, **E**xcretion, **F**eeding

♣ To remember wind direction in clockwise order ; **N**orth, **E**ast, **S**outh and **W**est:

- **N**aughty **E**lephants **S**pray **W**ater

♣ To memorise the seven countries in Central America; **B**elize, **G**uatemala, **E**l Salvador, **H**onduras, **N**icaragua, **C**osta Rica and **P**anama:

- **B**ig **G**orillas **E**at **H**otdogs, **N**ot **C**old **P**izza

11. Question timing, tactics and reading the paper:

a) Question timing: Make sure you are familiar with the following: How long is the paper? How many questions do I need to complete in each section and how long can I spend on each question? These are things you need to work out before each exam. Knowing your paper inside out and sticking to a time plan will minimise stress, especially when you reach the last thirty minutes.

b) Question tactics: Consider doing your best question first, second best second and so on. This will help settle the nerves and build your confidence. If there is a choice on a given paper, you need to have a cover question in case the option you have targeted doesn't work out. Start every new question on the left-hand side of a double page as the examiner will then be able to see the full question easier when totalling the marks and won't have to flick back and forward. Lastly, stick to the game plan you have for each exam paper. Great penalty kick takers over years of football always 'make up their mind and stick to it'.

c) Reading the paper: How you read an exam paper will influence how efficiently you answer it. Your eyes can play tricks under pressure, so make sure to read each question carefully and then read it again, watching out for punctuation. Pay special attention to words like "or" appearing in different places in a sentence, changing the meaning each time. Misreading a question is very common in state exams, for example, in History: Hitler's 'Foreign policy' is completely different to his 'domestic one'. If you misread something, unfortunately it is tough luck, so try not to launch into writing answers immediately without being sure what is being asked. You should plan essay style questions by creating a structured bubble plan or a mind map. This strategy is particularly useful in subjects like English, Irish, History and Home Economics (S&S) and these teachers will advise you more on this. A good way of ensuring you don't miss a trick on the exam paper is to run your finger under each word as you read it, especially if your reading skills aren't splendiferous.

12. **Writing the paper and most common exam mistakes:**

a) Writing the paper: Keep your handwriting as clear as you can, being aware that you tend to write quicker in exams and quality can suffer. If an examiner cannot read your writing, they must begin a deciphering process, possibly passing your script onto another examiner that can. Label each part of every question carefully e.g. 6 b (ii). If you cannot complete a part of a question, put a mark on the question paper and leave plenty of space in your answer book to come back to it later. Attempt everything on each paper as there are attempt marks for virtually every question which could be 2/5, 4/10 or even 12/20. Bear in mind that the examiner will be trying to give you marks and not take them away.

Show all your rough work on the paper, especially in the numerical questions. Never scribble anything out, instead put a line through it so it can still be read and corrected, as it could be worth marks. If you are struggling to write text to answer a question, using a picture or diagram can sometimes illustrate the point better and it can also help to simplify the problem. If you do draw a diagram, don't forget to label it.

You can use pencil on your answer book if you wish, but make sure it has a heavy nib with a clear mark and have spares ready. Personally, I wouldn't recommend using a pencil as it may become faded and unreadable if scripts are being sent back and forth to examiners for checking, however there is no law against pencil if that's what you're comfortable with.

Fully completing your exam paper is obviously critical, for example, if you only complete three of five questions, you are only going to be marked out of sixty percent for that paper, not one hundred percent. Leaving early should not be an option if you are taking your Leaving Cert seriously.

In relation to marking, you need to place twice as much emphasis and spend twice as much time on a part carrying fifty marks compared   to one offering twenty-five. A percentage of you reading this now will ignore this ACE tip, in spite of it being common sense. We all know the importance to reduce, reuse, and recycle these days and although it goes against my inner geographer, when writing the paper: don't save the trees.

Answering your paper neatly, skipping a line or two after each question is a sensible approach. Be aware that you can get extra paper as required by raising your hand. Similarly, graph paper is available in Maths, Geography and the Science subjects. When using graph paper, don't forget to write your exam number and the question number on it. This goes for any sheet of paper used during your exam.

b) Most common exam mistakes: From correcting exam papers myself over the years, here are five of the most common pitfalls I have found students stumble into:

i. Timing: Mismanaging your time in the exam hall can easily cost you a full grade and the biggest exam 'crime' is to leave do-able questions unattempted. It is a fact that it is easier to get the first twenty percent of the marks in any question than the last twenty. Therefore, if you find yourself stuck for time, do not spend it extending and perfecting an answer already done, keep moving. Move on to the last few questions, giving yourself an opportunity to assess them, even if your answer is sketched or in point form.

ii. Marking: It is important to be conscious of the marking scheme when you are time planning a question or question part. For example, in Maths you should spend twenty-five minutes on a fifty marker (always divide by two). You need to check the marks/timing balance in your other subjects and be clear on the tactics you will employ on the day. If the marks allotted to a question are small, then more than likely a few written paragraphs are sufficient as an answer. For these question parts, do not write an essay on the subject, even if you know loads about it, as there is only a maximum amount of marks you can attain. Be sure to include any rough work in your answer book. In fact, I don't think the phrase 'rough work' exists anymore, as any extra notes you write should be done on the same page, where the examiner knows it is part of that specific question part.

iii. Repeating yourself: When writing answers in your subjects, only make each point once. There are no extra marks for stating the same facts, even if you phrase them differently. From listening to examiners, they tell me that repetition is a very common mistake made by students. It just wastes time and is annoying. Sometimes on the exam paper, part of a question can be written on the next page and in the pressure of the moment; you don't see it and consequently leave it undone. To ensure this does not happen, be sure to read every single line on your exam paper and double check each printed page of it.

iv. Stay in context: When sitting a Language paper, it's not a good idea to drop in irrelevant quotations you have memorised. Quotes that you use need to be made in the context of the question. More than likely the question will not be phrased exactly the way you have prepared for, so you will need to be ready to adapt to whats being asked. I have noticed, when correcting exams, students will answer a question using information they know as opposed to answering what the question is asking. There is a placeholder entitled 'Worthless'(carrying zero marks) in most marking schemes for irrelevant material, so keep re-reading the question to make sure you stay on point.

v. Draw on your experiences: If I was writing an exam paper, I would draw on as many real life examples and personal experiences as I could, as I know the examiners look very favourably on these. A possible example would be writing an essay about a situation you found yourself in or a tough period of your life. These are the type of essays I chose in school myself. There is a sense of enjoyment in this type of writing, as you can easily bring yourself back to how you were feeling at that time and make the story feel real for the reader. Similarly, you will not have to rely on knowledge; instead you can tap into your own experience of the situation and write 'off the cuff'. A repeated word of warning here again though – while this creativity is to be encouraged – you need to be absolutely sure you have answered the question asked and not gone off on a tangent.

13. **Look after your eyes:** You will be doing plenty of reading from textbooks, summary notes, post-its, flashcards and the likes over the next few months, so it is important to look after your eyes during this period. The expert's advice on reducing eye strain is to apply the twenty-twenty-twenty rule. That is to take twenty seconds to look at something twenty feet away and repeat this every twenty minutes. Going outside on your breaks will get some fresh air to the eyes. Another good exercise is to simply rest your eyes in the palm of your hands for a few minutes, making sure that no light gets through.

14. **Learning off information:** In our modern Leaving certificate where you need to be able to apply knowledge to a topic; learning off too much information is a common mistake made by students and is not recommended. There is more of an emphasis now on applying your everyday life experience to each question. Similarly, if the butterflies are fluttering madly on the morning of the exam, you are less likely to remember a lengthy essay you have learned off. In my opinion, you are better off to stick with summaries, bullet points, post-its, quotes, mind maps, definitions, and little hardbacks. The Leaving Cert exam is

now more about identifying the important information in a question and discussing its merits, as opposed to emptying the contents of your head onto the answer book.

15. **Thinking critically:** I believe great students are those who can think critically about the information they have in front of them. To do this, you as a student should read the information presented by the author, understand it as best you can and then begin to question it critically. Being critical does not mean just being negative; it also means being knowledgeable and really assessing the quality of the information.

If you attend third level over the next few years, you will be expected to think on your own, evaluate/summarise information and make decisions about what content is useful and what is irrelevant. Getting into good habits now by practising critical thinking will enhance your leaving cert performance and be greatly beneficial going forward. My ACE tip here is to use your imagination, challenge the question being asked and don't be afraid to offer your own personal opinion on topics on the paper.

The Open University has developed a 'stairway' to help students understand the skills of critical thinking. Apply these steps to a specific topic in order to understand it better. I think this is an excellent way of studying, as you are reflecting on all aspects of the information presented. The steps are as follows:

- ♣ Process: take in the information (i.e. in what you have read, heard, seen, or done).

- ♣ Understand: comprehend the key points, assumptions, arguments, and evidence presented.

- ♣ Analyse: examine how these key components link together.

- ♣ Compare: explore the similarities and differences between the ideas you are reading about.

- ♣ Synthesise: bring together different sources of information to serve an argument or idea you are creating. Make logical connections between them.

♣ Evaluate: assess the worth of an idea in terms of its relevance to your needs.

♣ Apply: transfer the understanding you have gained and use in response to questions, assignments, and projects.

♣ Justify: use critical thinking to develop arguments, draw conclusions, and identify implications.

16. **Ways to stay calm prior to and during exams:**

♣ Breathe: If you feel anxious or feel like you are slightly losing control, it is a good starting point to take a few deep breaths while focusing on them. Focus on nothing else but the air slowly going in and out. This will help slow your heart rate down and aid calmness.

♣ The same boat: You need to keep in mind that you are probably not the only one struggling even though it feels like you are on your own. Talk to your friends about how they feel.

♣ Small steps: If you feel overwhelmed, don't make the classic mistake of thinking you must solve everything now. Focus on making a small step to get the ball rolling again.

♣ Keep it simple: I have found students over the years that overthink the exams, waste energy in nerves and tend to under perform on the day. Nervous energy is wasted energy and again deep breathing right down into the bottom of your lungs can help.

♣ Someone else's shoes: Another way to change your perspective in a tough situation is to get out of your own head. Do that by asking yourself, what would 'xxxxx' do in this situation? People like your parents or your calmest friend are good ones to consider.

♣ Don't leave it late: If you are the kind of person who arrives 'Just in time' for events, you need to alter your mind-set for the two weeks of the exams. Give yourself extra time in every journey to the exam hall otherwise your stress levels will go through the roof, remembering that there are many variables that can go wrong with our transport system in Ireland.

♣ Reduce, reuse, reduce: Reducing the amount of information on your lists, notes and exam aids will make you feel so much better. Creating summaries of the notes you have written makes content more manageable when it comes to revising later. Eliminating notes that are useless or irrelevant will have the same effect as tidying your room and you will feel like you are taking back control.

♣ Focus on the present: To remain more at ease, always think in the present and do a good job on what you are currently working on. When tomorrow comes, you have a different revision plan in place and you can deal with that then. Doing your best in the moment will leave you more contented and improve your focus.

♣ There will be blips: Part of the Leaving Cert process is realising obstacles will get in the way and things will not always run smoothly. The good students learn to accept interruptions and hurdles and just refocus on their next task. Your Lifestyle Timetable detailed in Chapter Two will help you get back on track.

♣ Be aware of how you are feeling: Being emotional, tired or angry about something will normally lead to poor quality study. If there is an issue in your life around exam time, be aware that you may need to build more breaks into your Lifestyle Timetable. Be good to yourself is the advice here. If you are in the middle of a study block and find yourself not even reading the words in front of you, it is time to do something different. Always listen to your body.

For more information on staying calm around exam time, see Chapter Four: Stress Busting the Leaving Cert.

17. **Be aware of the type of student you may be:** Knowing the type of student you are can help you plan your approach to exams better. Consider for a minute the type of student you might be:

Do you crave perfection? Do you believe you need every last percent? Keep in mind that there are back doors into courses and careers now, not like when I was young. Sometimes trying too hard can lead to underperformance. Take time for yourself; exercise, meet your friends and have fun.

Are you a high flyer? If you are taking extra subjects, you need to manage your time properly and share it equally among them. You also need to keep reminding yourself that it is a marathon not a sprint. Try not to put too much extra pressure on yourself as you may struggle to achieve your goals then.

Are you a grafter? If so, you need to be aware that even if you don't achieve maximum points, you have loads of other amazing qualities that the high achiever may not have. You should reflect your answers through your great personality traits and bring life experience onto the exam paper at every possible opportunity.

Are you an procrastinator? You need to get real and start preparing for your exams by putting your Lifestyle Timetable in place. You need to get familiar quickly with exam style questions from your past papers. Keep your options open and be aware that not everyone has to go to college. There are other possibilities available to you, namely; Post Leaving Cert (PLC) progression courses, Private colleges, UK or European courses, Apprenticeships, Youthreach or Colleges of Further Education to name but a few.

Are you usually in school? If you are the student who has missed a lot of time in school for whatever reason, it is important to be realistic. Depending on whether you are recovering from illness, bereavement or maybe a family issue, you just need to try and get back on track as best you can. I feel it should be said that there are more important things in life than exams, especially if you have lost someone close to you or if you have had a serious illness. Depending on your situation, it is amazing the amount of information you can process and how well you can end up doing in a short number of weeks. If I sat down to predict the exact grade my own students would achieve every year, I would guess very few of them perfectly. If you put your mind to it, you really can over-achieve, despite setbacks during the year.

You may recognise yourself in one of the above students, a combination of them or maybe you don't see any of these traits in yourself. However, you know your own strengths and the reality that you have it within yourself to step up and deliver as required. Always believe that you can reach deep into your reserves and ACE each exam paper with calmness and assurance no matter what type of student you are. See Chapter Nine for inspirational advice on how two former exam students found their final year journey.

18. **Know how to search google properly:** The Internet can be a great Educational resource for advice, tips, tricks, guidance and notes. I have downloaded hundreds of useful resources over the years that I use in my classroom and indeed to enhance my own knowledge every day. It is really important that you know how to use an Internet search engine like Google effectively. Here are a few simple operators that will help you get better results using Google:

♣ Quotations: Using quotations marks in your search terms lets you search exactly for the phrase you want. Your results will have that exact search term in them. Example: "Co-ordinate Geometry" will show up all web pages with Co-ordinate Geometry on it.

♣ Dashes: Use dashes if you wish to exclude something from your search. Example: Dogs-Dinner will show up all pages that have the word 'dogs' listed that don't mention the word 'dinner' in them.

♣ Tilde: Use tilde when you wish to search for a word or phrase and all other words or phrases that mean almost the same thing (synonym). Example: Maths~Classes will show up all pages that contain Maths classes, lessons, tuition etc.

♣ Site: Use site to search within a specific website only. Example: site: acesolutionbooks.com algebra will show up all references to algebra from my website.

♣ Vertical bar: Use a vertical bar to show up all pages that contain one, two or all terms. Example: Maths|Music|French will show up all pages with Maths, Music and French in them.

♣ Two dots: Use two dots to search within two number ranges. Example: German documentaries 2015..2017 will show up all German documentaries between 2015 and 2017.

19. **Write your notes by hand:** With a lot of schools switching to iPad's and tablets as a mode of education, the debate rages about which type of notes is the best to have from a classroom lecture i.e. typed or handwritten ones. As an ICT teacher myself, I still believe that the old fashioned way of taking notes by hand is the best for the following reasons:

♣ Since we now can type faster than we write, students are tending to type notes verbatim (exactly to the word) as they try to keep up with their lecturer. We are copying down a lot of the lecturer's language directly. There would be more of our own language than the lecturer's used in a handwritten set of notes, which makes them easier to understand and ultimately, of better quality.

♣ With handwritten notes, we spend more time thinking about the Information before the actual physical act of writing occurs. If we are attempting to type everything, there is less thinking time about that same information. In essence, I believe that slightly more learning takes place during the actual handwriting process.

♣ Keywords are the essence of any content. When you are taking down notes by hand in a lecture, you are listening out for the keywords to ensure you are grasping the bones of a sentence. Again, while typing you are trying to get everything down and so your brain misses out on this essential keyword focus.

♣ When handwriting notes, you are putting your own special stamp on them, making it easier to recall information you have translated into your own words.

♣ During a lecture, you can link up handwritten notes quicker with bubbles, arrows etc. and while doing this, you are learning what the connections and linkages are in the speakers' content.

20. **Record yourself:** With so many portable digital devices to play content on now, recording audio is a great option being availed of by many students. This is an excellent learning hack if you have long commutes or spend a lot of time in the car. Playing back notes you have recorded is a very successful method of retaining information. I have recorded questions and answers for job interviews previously, where I called out a possible interview question and then proceeded to answer it as best I could. Recording information on various subjects has been helpful during my career, when different jobs and challenges emerged. The nice thing about recording material is you can look at the possibility of a barter deal with your study buddy i.e. swap it for other audio content or even a great set of handwritten notes.

21.

ACE Inspirational Quotes

If you always do what you've always done, you'll always get what you've always got"
Henry Ford.

"Don't ever use the 'F' or the 'P' word
in my classroom... Fail or Pass"
Joe McCormack.

Chapter 6:

Exam Time = Feeding Time

Food provides all the essential nutrients that we require for healthy living and to fuel our physical activity. A car can work well, but if it doesn't have any fuel it can't go anywhere. Unfortunately for us, no single food provides all the nutrients required, so a mixture and range of different foods must be consumed in our diet. Research has shown that the healthier we eat, the better we feel and the more we can focus on tasks at hand. People who rely on sugary fixes too often, drink too much coffee or eat too much fatty foods are at risk of being sluggish, jittery, or feeling burned out. When studying for exams some students tend to stay up late and forget to eat and drink properly because of the stress or maybe worse, they eat too much of the bad stuff.

Poor eating habits before and during your exams will leave you with less energy both mentally and physically. To perform to your potential on the day, eating the proper food is essential. Eating small amounts regularly, avoiding junk and spicy foods can help avoid upset stomachs. It is not too late to start eating well, even with only a week to go before the exams. I have broken this chapter into easy to read sections about nutrition both at exam time and all year round.

The Key Nutrients

No matter what your diet is; vegan, dairy-free, vegetarian or carnivore, good nutrition will always keep you at your optimum health and help you concentrate better. So, what are the best nutritional and common-sense tips for healthy eating around exam time? To speak in general firstly, the food pyramid provides a representation of the different types of foods and the recommended number of servings of each. As a growing teenager, you need a good mix of these foodstuffs every day but you also need to be aware that some of these foods are more beneficial than others. The food pyramid contains the following nutrients:

♣ Carbohydrates - Bread, Potatoes, and Cereal.

♣ Fruits.

♣ Vegetables.

♣ Protein.

a) Meat, Fish, and Poultry.

b) Milk and Dairy Products.

♣ Fats.

In general, you need to plan ahead in relation to the foods you eat; this is especially relevant during pressurised exam times. One of the most important factors in good nutrition is to not allow yourself get too hungry, as hunger pangs tend to affect food choices. Have you ever noticed yourself buying a product in the supermarket that you didn't really need, while shopping on an empty stomach? People tend to go for what is convenient or nearby rather than what they require. When choosing your meals, there are a number of key factors to maintaining solid nutrition:

Wholesomeness - Choose fresh, wholegrain, whole wheat or lightly processed foods rather than packaged and refined foods.

Foods in their natural state nearly always have a higher nutritional value than processed foods.

Variety - If you find yourself with a repetitive diet, try to eat a different low sugar breakfast cereal, choose a different sandwich filling, or try different coloured vegetables.

Moderation - Try your best to eat foods in moderation.

The Food Pyramid

The food pyramid hypothesis recommends 'including a minimal amount of refined sugars and saturated fats, built upon a foundation of wholesome foods'. For you, your goal now is to build up the key nutrients in your body to cope with the levels of stress that occur during exams. Getting into good habits prior to your exam period ensures you have food working in your favour. With the experience of producing a nutritional guide for a county Gaelic football team, I want to pass on some of the knowledge I have gained through research and in my own life. More importantly, I hope the information will set you up for a healthy approach to nutrition, well after you graduate.

There is a misconception out there among teenagers (especially girls) that eating less will keep weight down. I believe that eating the correct foods, drinking plenty of water and doing moderate exercise is the way to go if you wish to maintain your weight or even lose a few pounds. Around exam time, you need to ensure you are well nourished and this includes having three solid meals every day. I will now look more closely at these three main meals to give you some ideas and concrete information about what you can include to boost your energy, concentration, and performance around exam time.

Breakfast

You have heard your parents and others say many times that "breakfast is the most important meal of the day" and that is a hard fact. A decent breakfast will give you energy to start each morning, help balance your weight and allow you to complete the tasks and challenges you face every day more efficiently. Breakfast is equally as important for children as it is for adults and a healthy one is a vital part of our health and wellbeing. The importance of breakfast as the first meal of the day has been scientifically proven; so your parents are actually correct. Imagine food is the fuel for your daily activity. During exams, your body will demand good quality clean fuel and regular refuelling in order to nourish itself and maximise your concentration, starting first thing in the morning.

I have my own experience in relation to eating breakfast. In my earlier career, I didn't eat anything in the morning until my first small break at work (eleven o'clock). During the early morning, I found myself regularly on edge and low in energy. I noticed that just before this break, my body was craving food. Basically, what was happening was my blood sugar levels had dropped too low and my concentration was poor during the first two hours of the day, and I knew it. As a teacher, I am familiar with students' eating habits in the morning as I see it in front of me every day. Maybe your stomach doesn't feel like food or is a bit unsettled that early in the morning. You may have eaten late the previous night and your stomach may be telling you that your body is still living off those energy stores. That's OK. But… just eat something, no matter how small, to kick-start your body again. If you think about it logically, your body has not fuelled up for eight to ten hours during the night, so denying it any longer makes no sense at all, especially from a blood sugar and an energy point of view.

My mornings now: In the last ten years, I have changed my early morning habits. I started eating breakfast and felt so much better for it. If you are that person that doesn't eat until eleven or twelve o'clock during the day: have a go at this food versus non-food trial. One day, try eating nothing until one p.m. and on the second day do the opposite, eating a reasonably sized breakfast before school. At lunch time on both days, write down how you are feeling, how much concentration you had in your early classes and how well you were able to participate in them. You will be surprised by the results.

From what I understand of research done, one of the best foods to eat for breakfast is porridge (oats). Porridge slowly releases energy into your body which gives a feeling of fullness, helping you concentrate longer, reducing the temptation to reach for junk food. Oats contain a significant amount of B vitamins, Iron and Magnesium. You can purchase pre-portioned and flavoured oats in stores, but I wouldn't recommend these due to the high amount of added sugars. Oatmeal can be boiled with water or milk and topped with fresh fruit, cinnamon, almonds or walnuts. You can also make overnight oats, which are soaked in milk or yoghurt for several hours so they are ready to eat in the morning. This would be my preferred breakfast option along with whole chia seeds, alpro soya yoghurt, organic honey and grapefruit or peach segments.

There are hundreds of breakfast options available that aren't that time consuming to prepare. These include: Smoothies containing fruit, plain yoghurt or chopped fruit with whole grain cereals and milk. A mixture like crushed nuts, a small dollop of organic honey and plain yoghurt can be quickly made and eaten. Homemade granola bars are great for when you're on the go, they are also better than the sugar-packed store-bought ones, and easier to make than you think. Personally, I would recommend the following foods for breakfast: Oats, Muesli, Grapefruit, Watermelon, Greek yoghurt, Smoothies, Wholemeal bread, Scrambled eggs, Bananas, Low sugar cereal, Actimel, Low sugar orange juice and Low sugar multivitamin juice.

If there are healthy wholesome foods you find hard to consume for breakfast, put other foods on top so that their unpalatable taste is masked. An example of this is to put bananas, fruit, yoghurt or honey on your porridge. I have found that my performance, energy, and concentration have improved greatly in school during the day, now that I have introduced porridge into my diet. I recommend you try it.

Parental role in the morning: Parents; if your child skips breakfast before school, they are more likely to be tired throughout the day and will have reduced concentration levels. As I have stated above, choosing a breakfast that is packed full of fibre, carbohydrates, grains, and protein will help boost their levels of concentration, improve memory, and will stop complaints of hunger as the morning progresses. If breakfast is a busy time of day in your house, then feeding your children what they need quickly might be a daunting experience, but it doesn't have to be. By stocking up on all the ingredients you need beforehand, you can deliver quick healthy breakfasts that they will enjoy. By preparing breakfast the night before, or getting them to prepare their own, you can cut wasted time in the morning. Alternatively, if your kids aren't hungry or everyone is in a rush out the door, make sure there are plenty of easy-to-grab pieces of fruit, yoghurt, smoothies, and muesli bars (sugar free) that can be eaten quickly or on the go. In an ideal world, everyone should sit down at the same time and share food together, although I do realise that this isn't always possible.

In the supermarket the other day, out of curiosity, I picked up a box of breakfast cereal. Its contents contained thirty four grammes of sugar for every one hundred grammes of cereal. This would be the equivalent of emptying the box and filling it one third (thirty three percent) full of sugar. If you give your children sugary cereals, high sugar juices or greasy fried foods in the morning, this is as bad as not feeding them at all. Pastries, pasties, and breakfast bars may look easy and appealing, but have pretty much zero nutritional value. Also, the high sugar content in many of these products will affect your child's performance during the day, as sugar gives energy quickly but does not have any long-lasting effect. With every high comes a low, and the high from the morning will cause the body to 'crash' once this sugar has run out and there is no other energy being released. You are doing your child a big favour by keeping sugar to the bare minimum in the morning, with sugary cereals and fruit juices being the biggest culprits.

Lunch

In the middle of the day, you need something that will sustain you until you get home from school. For lunch, I would recommend eating a sandwich of chicken, tuna, or turkey with a salad filling of your choice. I am not a fan of these large white bread rolls aka 'The chicken fillet roll', as the soft bread inside them doesn't appear to digest well. I often hear my students complaining of cramps in their stomach having had them for lunch; a coincidence maybe? But I doubt it! Eating too much for lunch can leave you feeling tired and sleepy, so I wouldn't really recommend a big dinner in the canteen or local café. Anyone who has had an afternoon slump knows what I mean. Try to eat a portion or two of fruit for extra Vitamin C to help fight common colds.

Again, as your exams get closer and you are studying at home, try and keep the same school routine. In other words, I would advise you to eat similar portions, and lunch, at the same time as what you did during term. It is very easy to get up late, skip breakfast and go to lunch, but this is quite an adjustment for your body to make. Your body will be used to eating certain foods at certain times so personally I wouldn't be introducing new foods or a new routine around exam time. I would recommend the following foods for Lunch: Beans, Salad, Brown rice, Yoghurt, Blueberries, Boiled vegetables, Bananas, Kiwis, Whole grain bread, Whole wheat bread, Chickpeas, Kidney beans, Leftover chicken, Tuna, Cottage cheese, Nuts, Healthy sandwiches, Packs of nuts, and Healthy wraps.

Dinner

In relation to the timing of dinner, I believe that you should try to eat this meal before seven-thirty p.m. to allow your body time to digest the food before bed. If your food is only partially digested, it may lie in your stomach leading to discomfort, as the body tries to break it down. The earlier you have your dinner, the more time the body has before bed to digest it. In my experience eating too late, especially carbohydrates can leave you feeling full and thus make sleeping more difficult. Fewer carbohydrates and more proteins (like fish, chicken, turkey etc.) at this time of the day are the way to go, as you don't need as much energy then.

In general, red meats have more cholesterol and saturated (bad) fat than chicken, turkey and fish. Cholesterol and saturated fat can raise blood pressure. The unsaturated fat in fish, such as salmon is called Omega-3 fatty acids and the experts tell us that it may reduce our risk of cardiovascular (heart) disease. It is worth keeping in mind that it is substantially easier to digest vegetables than meat and I believe the more vegetables you have on your dinner plate the better, no matter what these vegetables are. Personally, I find spinach, beans, peas, celery, green beans, cucumber, sweetcorn, olives, gherkins, chickpeas and celery great vegetables to include as part of this meal. Broccoli is also an excellent superfood for the body. It is rich in calcium, vitamin C, B vitamins, beta-carotene, iron, fibre and vitamin K. If you don't fancy broccoli, other vegetables such as cabbage are equally beneficial. If greens are not a runner in your house why not try Coleslaw? I find all of these above vegetables great for digestion, especially if I am eating dinner at six, seven or eight o'clock in the evening.

If you have fallen short of your five-a-day fruit and vegetables, try to include some fruit around dinner time if possible. This could be in the form of a starter or even a dessert. I sometimes squeeze the fresh juice of a lemon or lime on my dinner to increase fruit intake. These citrus fruits are full of Vitamin C and will fight any potential weaknesses developing in your system.

My Exam Nutrition Recommendations

The following are some general (and I hope useful) advice on good eating habits for the tough exam period and some useful information on future nutrition:

1. **Increase 'brain food' intake:** Proteins from lean meat, fish and eggs, fruit, nuts, and whole grains are foods that help keep the brain mentally alert. Snacking on nuts and dried fruit will help prevent concentration levels dipping. Keep in mind that fruit like bananas, blueberries, and oranges all have natural sugars that will give you a lift when you're feeling tired.

2. **Snack healthy:** When your head is in the books and time is ticking by, you might forget or skip a meal to keep up momentum. Your brain needs food and water to keep working and mental fatigue can cloud your brain, especially if an exam is close by. I would recommend the following healthy snacks to get you through study bumps: Whole wheat toast with peanut butter, fruit smoothies, yoghurt, berries, honey, dried fruit and nuts, hard boiled eggs, low fat chocolate milk, vegetables with dip or a low sugar granola bar.

    Large meals tend to leave us feeling stuffed and bloated. However, research shows that our energy levels start depleting three hours after we eat. Eating snacks are a great idea, as long as they are reasonably healthy of course. It is understandable that you may eat more than normal around this time but the most important thing is that your energy levels are high and nicely balanced throughout the day, especially on the days when you sit two exam papers. During these periods, graze away on the Guilt Free Good Stuff (GFGS).

3. **Minimise caffeine:** Caffeine is a stimulant that is present in coffee and many energy drinks. However, please be aware that you may only experience a temporary lift from them and there will be downtime thereafter. Too much caffeine can cause dehydration so if you're a coffee addict, try and cut back to one or two a day as it may cause mood changes, which are very unwelcome around exams. Sleep can also be affected by caffeine and I know a good few adults who abstain from caffeine after four p.m., as it disturbs their sleep. I would recommend water, peppermint tea or even a small glass of milk to aid sleep and as a healthy replacement for caffeine.

4. **Consume good fats:** You will notice that the fifth nutrient listed above is 'Fats'. Fats are an important component of the diet and have received an enormous amount of bad publicity over the last twenty-five years. Fat stores help fuel endurance because the store of

carbohydrate fuel is so limited in the body. More than any other nutrient, it is important to understand the different types of fats. Too much of one type or too little of the other can be harmful in your diet.

As a rough guide, saturated fats are generally solid at room temperature and tend to be animal fats (such as the fats found in butter or margarine). Butter itself contains approximately eighty-two percent fat with fifty-four percent of it being saturated. Unsaturated fats are liquid at room temperature and are usually vegetable fats (such as olive oil, rapeseed oil, oily fish (sardines, tuna, mackerel, or salmon)). Unsaturated fats or good fats are an important nutrient for you to intake as a student. The following are other sources of good fat fuel to keep the body ticking along: cheese, dark chocolate, eggs, nuts, coconut and coconut oil, peanut butter, pistachios and walnuts.

5. **Reduce added sugar:** Keeping sugars to a minimum seems so obvious these days, but we are all guilty of eating high fat, high sugar snacks when we are stressed out, such as muffins, chocolates, pastries and tarts. Studies have shown that foods with the combination of high fat and high sugar are the unhealthiest for us. These bad boys take our stomach extra time to digest and leave us feeling sluggish. If you have a sweet tooth, why not make a rare sugary treat part of a reward on your Lifestyle Timetable. I would say that it is OK to eat takeaways, sugary foods, fried foods etc. the very odd time but try and keep them to a minimum, more especially within a couple of weeks of the exams.

Without sounding like a kill joy, I would strongly recommend avoiding all fizzy drinks and the so called 'energy bars'. You should always look at the amount of sugar for every one hundred grammes of weight in these bars, remembering there are three grams of sugar in a teaspoon. Almost all digestibles will now list the amount of nutrients present per one hundred grammes, making it a lot easier to compare products for sugar, salt and fat content.

Data from the National Health and Nutrition Survey in America shows that the average teenager ingests twenty-eight teaspoons of added sugar a day. These statistics are shocking with Irish teenagers moving towards these levels also. I would strongly encourage you to start reading labels on your food. Any food with more than fifteen grams of sugar per hundred grams of product weight is said to be high in sugar. The World Health Organisation (WHO) has stated recently that the average teenager should intake 6.5 teaspoons of added sugar every day. Table 1 shows some examples of how much sugar certain products now contain. Looking at the 330ml regular can of coke below; consumption of it sends a teenagers' daily intake of sugar over the recommended amount by one third. I don't think elaboration of this point is required due to its starkness.

Table 1: Percentage of Recommended Daily Intake of Added Sugar for a Teenager

Product	Teaspoons of added sugar	% of Recommended daily intake of sugar
A medium muffin	Eight	123%*
A regular can of coke	Nine	138%*
Regular slice of cake	Fourteen	175%*
Hot chocolate with marshmallows and cream	Eighteen	276%*

*100% is the recommended daily amount of added sugar per day for a teenager.

6. **Target one or two improvements:** Rather than aiming to overhaul your diet, start by targeting one specific area for improvement before your exams. This should be something that is most relevant to you and is the easiest thing to change, for example, breakfast. If you are someone who doesn't eat a healthy breakfast, you could start by prioritising that. As you become more consistent with that meal, you can work on another area like eating more fruit and vegetables or reducing sugary drinks. It is important to be realistic about what you wish to achieve and give yourself some weeks before the exams start to achieve it.

Progress on any changes made should be judged over several weeks, rather than days, as new habits take time to form. Get a shopping list together and ask your parents to stock the fridge and freezer with your targeted foods for the six weeks. Also, if you can do a bit of cooking for yourself, you will never go hungry. Of course, remember that if you fall off the horse with tempting treats, just get back on again and tally ho! Any minor improvements in the quality of food that you consume should lead to better concentration for study. You probably won't believe me until you make some alterations, so start today.

Whether you are studying or about to take an exam, eating right, carrying healthy snacks, and drinking plenty of water will greatly aid concentration levels and give you lots of energy. In general, it has been proven that a poor diet will affect your sleep, your mood and will leave you struggling to focus. I recommend you try preparing some healthy snacks at home. Ask your parents about homemade popcorn, chilled water with lemon/lime, little vegetable pieces with tomato dip, fruit plates of melon / grapes / kiwis / strawberries / raspberries, flavoured corn cakes or even some plain biscuits.

7. **Hydrate very well:** Firstly, it's important to know that your weight affects your fluid needs. You should drink 35ml of fluid daily for every kilogramme you weigh. For example, a 70kg (11.02 stone) person should drink 2.45 litres per day. In athletes, research has shown that a two percent drop in hydration can lead to up to thirty percent drop in performance.

Water is the best form of hydration and the benefits of water are well documented. Water increases energy, flushes out toxins, improves skin complexion, boosts the immune system, prevents cramps, balances the body's fluids, promotes digestion, and eliminates waste products. Having all these benefits working in your favour around exam time is only going to help you. Low sugar fruit juices, like cranberry, blueberry and apple are good for hydration and contain enzymes and vitamins. Fizzy drinks will also hydrate but again are to be avoided due to their high sugar content. Other foods to improve hydration include: Cucumbers, Watermelon, Pineapple, Tomatoes, Blueberries, Pear, Grapefruit, Lettuce, and Melon. Ultimately, sipping on water throughout the day is the best way to avoid dehydration.

If you get dehydrated, your study at home and your concentration in class will suffer. Here are four tell-tale signs that your body is dehydrated and that you need to drink more fluids:

- ♣ Dry mouth and skin: If you are dehydrated you may not be producing enough saliva which will lead to a build-up of bacteria in the mouth. You also may see acne appearing.

90

♣ Food cravings: The body confuses thirst for hunger sometimes. Drinking water will reduce these cravings as it is water your body often requires not food.

♣ Headaches, tiredness, and confusion: A lack of water can lead to headaches during the day. This makes it very difficult to operate to your maximum capacity. Ask yourself the question, "Am I constantly tired?" If the answer is yes, you might just be lacking water in your diet. The process of learning and retaining information has been proven to be more difficult if your body lacks fluid.

♣ Dark coloured urine: The colour of your urine should be light if you are hydrated and a dark colour indicates the opposite. The average hydrated person goes to the toilet to excrete urine between six and eight times a day.

To combat dehydration, you should bring a bottle or water with you to school every day. Keeping bottles of cold water in the fridge at home will make it easy to 'grab and go' and you can sip away on it as the day progresses. The recommended daily amount of water for a teenager is two litres which works out at eight to ten glasses; however, I would recommend that you drink more if the day is particularly hot or if you are exercising. It is important to note that if you feel some of the above listed symptoms, your body may already be dehydrated. Prevention is better than cure in this case.

8. **Power up energy levels:** You need loads of energy around exam time. The nights before exams are quite tiring as you are concentrating more than ever and this is not to even mention the exam paper itself. To keep the energy levels up, I would recommend consumption of the following foods: Honey, Apples, Spinach, Almonds, Yoghurt, Beans, Oats, Sweet potatoes, and Eggs. These are better eaten in the morning to lunch-time period, as according to research the body is more suited to digesting them at this time. Every person's digestive system is different, so try them and see which ones work best for you.

9. **Avoid alcohol:** As you approach the age of eighteen, it's important to be aware how alcohol can affect you. Alcohol has a high-energy content and it takes the liver a long time to break it down. Alcohol is

not an effective energy source for working muscles and a high weekly consumption of alcohol may provide energy above an individual's requirements, but not in a good way as this energy will be stored as fat. Alcohol kills brain cells, blocks the absorption of water and will have a negative effect on your body clock, ultimately affecting study. Of course, the purchase or consumption of alcohol for anyone under eighteen is illegal.

ACE Inspirational Quotes

"If you can keep your head when all about you are losing theirs and blaming it on you"
Rudyard Kipling.

"Be the best at what you do.
Use the tools of your trade,
if it's books or a floor to dance on
or a body of water to swim in.
Whatever it is, it's yours"
Michael Jackson.

Chapter 7:

Exam Day is Here!

You have prepared well, have completed your Lifestyle Timetable over the last number of weeks, your diet has improved and your water consumption is excellent. You are now almost ready for day one. With a week to go before the exams start, you will more than likely be at home driving your parents mad and them you too. Since you won't be in school during the day, a full Lifestyle Timetable is vital to make the most of your time (See Chapter Two for how to implement it). It is advisable to keep the same routine as you had during school time, starting with getting up and finishing with going to bed at the same time. Minimising adjustments your body has to make, will help it be ready for the first day of the exams. Stick to your plan and try and eat and exercise as you have been doing. Four to six hours study per day during this time should be enough, assuming you have all your preparation notes in place. Breathing deeply right down into your lungs will help nerves and paying attention to hydration in the final week is important. (Chapter Six will tell you more about the importance of hydration).

At this point now you will not have any set classes in school making it more important to be self-motivated. Your subject teachers will still be available to you and I would highly recommend going in and talking to them if you need any final advice or have a question about the course; this will set your mind at ease and they will be more than happy to help you. If the weather is good, try and get out for some walks etc. I wouldn't sit out in the sun directly, as coping with sun burn in an exam hall is a nightmare. It is absolutely fine to lie out somewhere quiet in the shade and do some revision, just bring a bottle of water with you.

Having negotiated the 'Home Study' period, you are now ready for take-off, as thoughts turn to the exam hall. Questions floating around your head at this stage might include: Are the exam number lists up in school? What exam centre will I be in? Where will I be positioned in the exam centre? Will all my class be in the one exam centre? Or what's the weather going to be like over the next few weeks? These are all secondary concerns and will look after themselves in the fullness of time. To perform to your best, knowing what to expect in the exam hall is important; the exam hall procedures and 'etiquette' adopted for the Junior Cycle exams are now a distant memory. This chapter will present some final guidelines and remind you of exam day from start to finish and all that it entails.

Before Leaving the House

The morning of the exam, especially the first morning can be a tense time for everyone. The night before may not have been your best night's sleep ever, but that's normal enough. You will sleep better the night after the first day is over, all going well. On a given exam day, I wouldn't be getting up too early especially if you have an exam that afternoon; you will just be shattered tired. Personally, I would advise you to do around thirty to forty-five minutes revision at home before leaving for the exam centre. During this time, I would be revising summarised notes in the form of a mind map, post-its, flash cards or a summary notebook. The morning of the exam is not the time to be looking at any new material; stick to your guns and trust the processes and summaries you have put into place over the last few months.

Before leaving the house, have a good breakfast (more information about the importance of breakfast is contained in Chapter Six). You need to be at the exam centre at least thirty minutes prior to all your exams so if you are travelling, give yourself extra time in case there is a traffic accident, bad weather or an unforeseen event. During the exam period, you shouldn't be 'Just in time' for any exam, therefore I would strongly advise leaving home early and so taking that potentially stressful situation out of play. If you are a last-minute type of person, be diligent, making sure your parents are on the ball if they are driving you there.

Without stating the obvious, make sure to double check the time of each exam. Put a copy of the exam timetable up in your room and highlight your exams. Give a photocopy of this marked exam timetable to your parents to keep them in the loop. There have been cases of pupils forgetting to go to an exam or worse still, sleeping through it. The finish time for an exam is as important as the start time. There have been situations where students thought that they had another thirty minutes left in an exam, when the superintendent called time. Believe it or not, these types of scenarios occur every year around the country. Make sure you have all your materials for each exam. In other words, double check exactly what's in your bag each day. Make sure you have a second black/red pen, eraser, pencil, water, any other required instruments and a few sweets to stay cool.

Arrival at School

School on the morning of an exam isn't going to be a great place for revision. On arrival, you will observe some students on edge as the anticipation heightens. Not a brilliant environment for last minute study, is it? However, if you feel like you need to take some cards or summaries with you, do so. I wouldn't be bringing wads of notes as you will only freak yourself out thinking "I didn't spend enough time on this" or "I don't know half of what's in this textbook" etc. I would ignore any stray comments from your peers like "This is coming up..." or "Have you heard that...?" etc. Even your own well-meaning friends can derail you. Being an exam superintendent myself, I arrive early to school on day one and see the shenanigans some students engage in. Keep in mind that the exam paper was set back in autumn, so rumours in person or on social media are just that – rumours. Keep your focus and stay in the present as best you can, believing in what you have prepared to your utmost ability.

Avoiding conversations about the paper just before you enter the exam hall is a good idea. You might be clear and confident in your head about topics studied and some throwaway comment can put doubts in your mind. Another issue can be if someone mentions a topic that you may not have studied in-depth and suddenly you are wondering "Will this appear on the paper?" At this late stage, stick to your guns, trust yourself and stroll in with your head held high. I believe you are better served using that walk to get your mind ready, rather than chatting to your friends. Topics discussed, prior to the exam may not appear anyway, so worrying about something that may never happen is energy wasted. I would advise using the toilet just before start time, as the chances are you will be hydrating that morning.

I have spoken extensively in previous chapters about the value of exercise in this book but it's not something you would normally associate with the morning of an exam. You might consider a walk or a short jog on the morning of the exam; a walk to school is ideal if you live nearby. Dr. Chuck

Hillman of the University of Illinois has provided evidence that twenty minutes exercise before an exam can boost memory and improve performance. Interesting research indeed!

Twenty Last Minute Guidelines

With days to go before your exams, here are some short term guidelines to keep you on task and focused in your preparation:

1. With only a short period left in school, it is important not to get too sucked into the end of year celebrations. However, you should enjoy and participate in them as reaching the end of second level is important and is a big milestone in your life.

2. Remain in school right to the end of term until your teachers indicate that they have reached the end of class teaching time. Do not be tempted to stay at home studying until classes actually finish. My view here is that you will be long enough at home studying and your teachers may inspire you with some last-minute experience. When timetabled classes finish, get up at the same time as you normally do each day so that you are maximising your time. If you stay on in bed, you may find motivation waning and half the day over when you get up.

3. Re-do a realistic Lifestyle Timetable (See Chapter Two). With a week to go, only plan your lifestyle timetable three days ahead as you might find yourself making more or less progress than expected and may need to change course. As previously stated, be sure to include exercise, rest, meals and breaks on this timetable. Check in with your parents to see if there are any important events you need to go to over the next few weeks making sure they are fully aware that exam preparation is the priority.

4. If you have not already done so, draw up a list of topics that you need to revise in each subject over the next few weeks. Use past examination papers and your text books to ensure you have the full list of topics required for each subject. Associating a specific topic with a past exam question will reinforce the importance of this topic

later. Noting the question number and year examined beside the corresponding topic is also a good idea.

5. It isn't advisable to engage in long discussions with your friends about planned study sessions. Hearing about the vast reams of study they are planning to get through will only make you feel worse or maybe even make you feel you are not doing enough. Students are usually not doing all they say they are. Even if they are putting in long days, this doesn't necessarily mean the quality of their preparation is good.

6. Study smart, by actively learning with the highlighter and red pen. This will help you focus on the key points as they appear on the page. The important thing is to stay switched on, otherwise nothing is going in and its just reading meaningless words on a page.

7. Summarise chapters from textbooks in the minimum amount of words possible and then try an exam question based on the content you have produced. I feel it is seriously important to have a set of notes that you have written yourself being clear on the train of thought through them from start to finish.

8. Try to be fair to all subjects and give them equal time. As I found myself in school, it was tempting to spend more time on subjects I liked or was good at doing, for example Technical Drawing and Maths. Despite me spending a disproportionate amount of time on Technical Drawing, I didn't go on to complete further studies in it, so you never really know how things will pan out.

9. Ask your teacher for a soft copy of the most recent Examiners' report for your subjects. These useful documents give advice on answering questions, errors previous students made, sample answers and recommendations for the future. They are all available online for viewing. Copper fasten your familiarity with the layout of each paper in your subjects and be fully aware of the instructions listed on them to avoid any structural surprises on the day.

10. I wouldn't get too much into the business of cutting corners or predicting what will come up. Your teachers have already advised you during the year what content is important, so re-familiarise yourself

with this. Create a section in your summary notebook to record any information in class that your teachers give you in relation to these insights. Cutting corners and predictions can be a dangerous game.

11. In your preparation, it is important to stay positive and know that the marking schemes for each paper are written in your favour. Any reasonable step in the right direction or partially correct answer will warrant some marks. Many subjects' marking schemes have been tweaked over the years to allow students more opportunities to pick up marks and demonstrate their knowledge of a subject.

12. Speak to your parents and siblings about your exams, explaining to them the type of environment you need at home for those few weeks. Tell your parents what you need in relation to food, space, support etc. This will help them prepare for what's ahead, as it may be their first time going through the process.

13. Have a look at any late-night habits you may have. Hours on your phone in bed isn't great exam preparation, as it will disturb sleep. The body performs better in a routine and so changing it as exams approach doesn't work well. You had a nice little routine that you settled into during term time, so I recommend sticking with that.

14. Students often ask me about the balance between revising material covered and preparing new content. Firstly, you have taken a lot of information in over the last two or three years, more than you would have imagined. How you present this knowledge in your answer book on the day is important, so I would advise you to work on your presentation techniques including layout, structure, neatness, conciseness, and organisation. Personally, I would advise against taking on large swathes of material to revise at this stage, instead it is better to build on your existing knowledge.

15. Use the study buddies (your friends) that you have worked with on different subjects over the year. Even with one week to go; write notes for each other, have discussions, meet up for coffee and bounce ideas off each other. Sitting down in a gang of three and brainstorming a topic is a brilliant idea, as you will have plenty of topic knowledge to share with each other at this stage of the year. The idea is that you will be in the exam hall and think "Yeah xxxxx

said that the other night". You will then need to put their information in the context of the question being asked on the day. Much research has proven that the best way to retain information yourself is to teach that said material to someone else. I can vouch for this as every time I teach something, I learn something new also.

16. It is useful to know that your teachers will be available for questions, discussions and advice around exam time. However, during the last few days prior to the exams, your teacher may be at home. I would recommend leaving a message with the secretary of your school if you wish to get in touch with them. As exams approach, our minds are more focused and are more in tune with Information we should be passing on to you to help you.

17. If at this stage you have very little study and preparation done, all is not lost. Starting study with one week to go beats the hell out of starting with two days left and when the exams start you will be studying every night anyway. Your plan now should totally focus on the upcoming week and how you can maximise use of it. Have a read of Chapter Two for details on how to construct your Lifestyle Timetable.

18. Being super organised will help you feel so much better. Setting out your notes in topic bundles will put things in perspective and these can be easily picked up as you need them. The fewer notes you have to revise now at this point, the better. Organising your notes and summaries will give you feelings of being in control. "You got this" so...Organise, Summarise and Consolidate.

19. A certain level of anxiety and worry will be normal as exams approach. My Stress busting tips in Chapter Four might be a useful read at this point, where I have detailed strategies and techniques to help you manage increased stress levels. I would recommend you have some techniques in place to help with anxiety if it appears. Remember the calmer you are, the more focused you will be on your organisation and content. Above all if you are feeling anxious, make sure and talk to your friends or family to see how they can help you work it out. As the advertisement explains, "It's OK not to feel OK and it's OK to ask for help."

20. Keep in mind that all past exam papers and marking schemes are available online to download from the Internet. I would highly recommend that you check out the process and thinking behind how each paper is marked. You should investigate things like: how to pick up attempt/credit marks, how the weighting of the marks is balanced, and most importantly what is the minimum standard required in questions in order to reach a certain grade. A solutions book where each step is detailed is an excellent companion to this research. Examples of such books can be viewed on www.acesolutionbooks.com. Being familiar with how papers are marked and the process of getting to a solution will arm you with information most students won't have and this is especially important if your teacher didn't get an opportunity to discuss it with you in class. Focus firstly on the SEC past exam papers, as these are the official ones asked in previous years. After you are confident on these, you can then move on to various unofficial sample papers.

My Twenty Five Exam Hall Diamonds

From my own secondary school experience followed by years of difficult college exams, I've spent a nice bit of time in exam halls picking up great experience sitting Maths, ICT and Geography papers along with various Educationally themed ones. These are some of the techniques and shortcuts that worked for me during my study days. Every year, I try to pass as many of these on to my own students as their exams approach:

- ♣ Lay out your answer book as clearly as possible.

- ♣ Put a box around each answer to make it easier for the examiner to identify and correct.

- ♣ Never leave a question answerless. You can very easily gain marks for making even the most basic attempt.

- ♣ The method you use to answer a question is more important than the answer you arrive at.

- ♣ Double check how many marks each individual part of a question is worth on the day and give it an appropriate amount of time.

♣ Write down any formulas, acronyms or key pieces of information you have memorised the minute you sit down in the exam. In doing this, you can empty your head of content instead of risking not recalling it later.

♣ Start by briefly reading through the questions and make some notes on the paper of what jumps into your head in relation to the topics that you recognise.

♣ Keep re-reading a question if you are unsure about what is being asked. Surprisingly, a large percentage of students only read a question once and then tear into it. Some of these students end up answering a question they think is on the paper as opposed to the question that is actually written there. Be on your guard here as the examiners will have no sympathy for those you don't address what's being asked.

♣ If the question requires a step-by-step approach for a solution, make sure to write every single step down in your answer book. This especially applies to subjects like Home Economics (S&S), Maths, Geography, and Physics etc. This will ensure you get the majority of the marks even if you make a little mistake at the end.

♣ When answering questions in different subjects, be aware of how the marking works on each exam paper and tailor your answer appropriately. For example, Languages will be marked on structure, layout, content, and vocabulary; where in contrast, Maths will be marked on attempts and steps in the right direction.

♣ Draw diagrams where possible to make your point. If you are more of a visual learner, you will be good at enhancing your argument with diagrams. Make sure and label each diagram well and refer to it in your text paragraph.

♣ Remember there is often more than one way to find an answer in certain subjects, so don't be afraid to experiment and express yourself if you're not fully sure what to do. Examiners love individuality and expression.

♣ Show all your workings within a question. Do not do rough work somewhere else in your answer book where the examiner may not understand its importance. Most exam papers now allow you to write the answer in a box or grid, so you should show all your workings there. Any work done in your head or on your calculator should be written down on your answer book.

♣ I would advise against the use of Tippex. If you wish to erase something, just put an 'X' through it, making sure it is still visible. Examiners must correct everything on the paper including information that has been crossed out, so this content could in fact be worth marks.

♣ When answering a question based on a graph, draw lines on the graph to show your readings, as you could lose marks for just writing down the answer only. This mainly applies to the Social Science subjects like Maths, Geography, Science, and Physics etc.

♣ Always have an idea in your head of the order you plan to attempt each question on a paper; remembering how exam papers can differ between subjects. Consider setting aside time for reading at the start, reviewing at the end, and also dealing with longer questions that carry different marks. These considerations depend on the subject. Speak to your subject teacher to formulate a plan here.

♣ I would start each paper by doing my best question first and finish with my 'not so good' question last, while constantly watching the time. This will allow you to control the paper and not the other way around. If you leave a question you are confident on until the end and time somehow conspires against you, you may not even get to it.

♣ Put your hand up and ask for extra paper if you run out of space for part of a question. Ensure to indicate which question it is on the new sheet. Leave space between each question part. A neat exam paper makes a good impression with an examiner.

♣ Do not leave an exam early even if you think you've done all you can. You'll be surprised with the extra information you can add in, once you start checking over each question. You should stay and work until the end of the exam as you owe it to your family, teachers, and school; but most of all you owe it to yourself for all the long hours you have spent preparing. As an exam superintendent every year, I see students going back checking pages, making minor changes and adding things in, right until the end.

♣ Take time to read, understand, and answer the questions that are being asked of you. Highlighting or underlining the keywords will help you focus on the key elements of the question. Be very careful not to misread a question.

♣ Learning information off is not recommended. In every subject, there is a fair chance that questions will not be asked exactly the way you have prepared them. In all exams, you need to cleverly adapt your answer; otherwise, it may be viewed as deliberately not answering the question. Consider this: you would not demonstrate a hill-start during your driving test when asked to do a turning manoeuvre.

♣ Every exam paper will have its own marking scheme. This grading scheme will have been set by an official from the department and approved by an external examiner. Simply put, if you do not address the points on the marking scheme you will not do well. In preparation for your exams, you should familiarise yourself with a typical exam marking scheme for each subject. By failing to answer the question asked you are showing an apparent lack of knowledge for the subject.

♣ You are likely to be nervous when it comes to the morning of your exam. Nerves and adrenaline can contribute to you forgetting information learned off. I have seen students forget reams of lines from a piece of work they have memorised, and then panic. It is not something anyone wants to see (even the toughest examiners), so it is strongly recommended not to spend time learning off essays or large chunks of text. Identify key information for each sub-topic and adapt this intelligently to the questions being asked on the paper.

♣ If you finish an exam earlier than expected, go back and revisit the questions you left unfinished (the ones you should mark with an '*'). If you run out of time, just fire down something on the page for any questions unattempted, making sure to label your attempt with the number of the question. On the off chance that you have timed the paper poorly, don't be afraid to jot down some bullet points for a question part before time is called.

♣ Focus totally on your own work in the exam hall, taking your time reading questions. Formulate answers before writing them down and stay concentrated until the superintendent says "stop".

"There are no regrets in life, Just lessons."

Jennifer Anniston

Exam day Quick Reference

Here is a quick reference list of 'one liners' that you can look down through the night before your first exam:

♣ Do your best – that is all that is expected of you.

♣ Get to the exam hall at least fifteen minutes before each exam.

♣ Be fully aware of the start and finish time of each exam.

♣ Read the instructions carefully on the paper.

♣ You cannot leave during the first thirty or the last ten minutes.

♣ Prepare for a longer exam paper than any of your school exams.

♣ Make sure you have plenty of pens, pencils, rulers, etc.

♣ Phones, books and notes are all forbidden in the exam hall.

♣ Use the toilet before entering the exam hall.

♣ Answer your best question first to settle the nerves.

♣ Take your time when reading each question.

♣ Attempt all parts of every question asked.

♣ If you make a mistake, draw a line through, so it is still readable.

♣ Questions answered, even if cancelled out, must be corrected.

♣ Check that you have answered all parts of all questions.

♣ Make sure to include all extra pages used e.g. graph paper.

♣ If you wish to use a pencil, make sure you use a dark one.

♣ Place twice as much emphasis on ten markers than fives etc.

♣ Carefully label any diagrams you draw or use.

♣ Layout your paper well. You can save the trees in later life.

♣ Do not repeat yourself in a question.

♣ Skip a line or two after each full question.

♣ Remember that any reasonable attempt will get you some marks.

♣ Bring some sweets and water into the exam hall.

♣ Focus on your own work not your friends work beside you.

♣ Don't panic if you don't understand a question at first.

♣ Eat good meals before and after each exam.

♣ If you run out of paper, ask for more from the superintendent.

♣ Put your exam number on all sheets you hand up.

♣ Think how your answers will sound to someone else reading it.

♣ Spend time on a question depending on marks allocated.

♣ Try and write clearly especially in subjects with a lot of writing.

♣ Answer the exact question that you are being asked on the paper.

♣ Go into each exam with a positive and determined attitude.

♣ Put a '*' on questions you didn't finish and revisit at the end.

♣ Show all rough work for each question on your answer book.

♣ A labelled picture/diagram can explain better than words.

♣ Scribble down notes if you happen to run out of time.

♣ Stay until the end of all your exams.

♣ Do your best!

Administration Information for the Exam Hall

If you are just about to sit your Junior or Leaving Cert exams, the following administration information is certainly worth a quick read beforehand. The more familiar you are with exam hall procedures, the more you can focus on your own game plan:

1. Be very clear on the timing of each exam.

2. Get there early on the first day of your exams to find out where to put your school bag and what centre (room) you are sitting in.

3. Sit at the table where your exam number is displayed.

4. Double check you are happy with your chair and table on arrival.

5. When you sit down each day, double check you have the correct paper and label in front of you. At Leaving Cert level, you can change from one level to another on the morning of the exam but this does

not come recommended, as you have spent considerable time studying a specific level.

6. On day one, the Superintendent (the person supervising your exams) will read out a shortened version of the rules and regulations.

7. You cannot bring any notes, school bags, phones or materials into the exam hall with you. You should just bring in your pens, instruments and some water/sweets.

8. For certain exams, don't forget to seal section A and Section B inside your answer book if you write on them. You can tie all your exam material together at the end using the stationary provided.

9. For the Aural (Listening) CD, make sure and tell the superintendent if you cannot hear the CD clearly. In most languages, the aural and the written exam will run one after the other. This will be clearly detailed on your exam timetable anyway.

10. Listen to the superintendents' instructions carefully at the start of each exam, as there may be corrections to be made to the exam paper or other announcements.

11. Be aware that Higher, Ordinary and Foundation Papers may finish at different times.

12. The finish time for all exam papers is written on the front of the paper.

13. Graph, tracing, and isometric grid paper are available on request from the Superintendent.

14. If you break the rules in the exam, you may not be allowed to sit another state exam again and may forfeit your remaining exams.

15. You will not be allowed enter the exam hall once thirty minutes from the official start time of the exam has elapsed.

16. If you take Paper one at Higher level for a subject, you must take Paper two at Higher level also. The same obviously applies to Ordinary and Foundation levels.

17. You can obtain a copy of the exam paper from the school authorities after an exam is over. The exam papers and their marking schemes will be uploaded to the examinations website soon thereafter also.

18. Do not be afraid to ask the superintendent if there is any issue you need help with, even something as small as requiring a tissue etc.

19. Ensure you write your exam number on all your writing material.

20. You will be informed when you have five minutes left in each exam.

ACE Inspirational Quotes

"I believe in you"
Kylie Minogue.

"If at first you don't succeed,
read the question"
Sean Mansfield.

Chapter 8:

Case Study - 'Here is how you prepare for...Maths'

As you prepare for your final exams, teachers and parents totally understand that even though you are making great strides, you still have plenty of fears. From talking to students, I find it's not the full set of exams that cause concern; it is usually only one or two subjects. Naturally everyone has their own talents and subjects they prefer. Personally, I was better at the Sciences than the languages but I persevered and got the grades I wanted in the languages I chose.

Sometimes subjects you are not looking forward to are the ones that have you on guard and you end up doing better in; A paper on the day can go well in an exam you were dreading. I regularly hear welcome surprise coming from students on results day, with comments such as "I didn't expect that result in xxxxx". The moral of the story here is that too much concern about a subject could end in false worry and be draining you of energy; energy you need for studying and getting your head right. Preparing for one of your less favoured subjects is a blatant case of having to 'get on with it' i.e. 'Eating your Frog' again. Of course, it is easier to study and work on subjects you enjoy and are good at, but you must not ignore the others. Studying and preparing the 'frog subjects' is probably the biggest challenge you will face during your Leaving Certificate year. Author and reconstructive surgeon, Jack Penn, once said:

> "One of the secrets in life is making stepping stones out of stumbling blocks".

Prioritise the Subject

In order to deal with a subject you find difficult, you need to prioritise it on your Lifestyle Timetable. It should therefore be ranked in your top three subjects and entered first onto the timetable with the possibility of including more study blocks for it than other subjects (See Chapter Two for more details on this). In these subjects, you need to: ask for plenty of help from your teacher, work with a study buddy, find ways of learning that best suits you, break it into manageable chunks, write a good set of notes that you can relate to and understand, think outside the box and ultimately dig in and persevere. These are all the characteristics of successful students.

"Someone once told me not to bite off more than I could chew; I said I'd rather choke on greatness than nibble on mediocrity"

Unknown

Grasping a Subject of Difficulty

In my experience, one of the subjects that students have most difficulty preparing is Maths. Maths seems to have developed a 'bad boy cred' over the last twenty years, but I feel things are getting better slowly and I know students feel more positive about it since the introduction of Project Maths in 2008. In general, I think students are enjoying the more practical approach in the subject since the changes. The existing course is however still quite long and you need to box clever in order to pin it down. I believe you can learn to grasp key concepts without being born a Maths genius. People regularly ask me about this hypothesis and I believe Maths is a subject everyone can do well in by being more open minded and willing to try different methods. For sure, your parents have a role to play here, so make sure and get them involved.

During this chapter, I will try to enrich you with information to master my subject. I will also provide you with some tools and ideas to tie parts of the Maths course together. More importantly though, I intend to impart my extensive experience of the subject, which should help to sharpen your focus on it. The advice given in this chapter will be beneficial for Maths, but will also be useful for other subjects that you may be struggling to come to terms with. Many of the principles discussed below are ones of finding the best way to understand a subject you don't really fancy.

Maths: Learning by Doing

To me, Maths is a subject where you need to be continuously 'learning by doing' and the importance of attempting exam style questions cannot be underestimated. Reading through questions and text like you do in other subjects will not work in Maths and having access to a structured solution book for exam questions is important. Inevitably with some challenging questions in the subject, you will run into difficulties getting started and this is where having the first line or two of the solution can be extremely helpful; a detailed solutions book is ideal for this. I believe that referring to the first part of a solution and then revisiting the question yourself is a very efficient way of developing key Maths skills. This technique isn't one much practiced in other subjects. You must adopt a different approach to maths; it is unique.

A genuine attempt to start a question in Maths will allow you to gain some momentum and progress to apply the concepts you have learned in class. In my experience, the biggest stumbling block to achievement in Maths is getting the question started; but a single grain of rice can tip the scales. In general, if you are finding it difficult to get started and feel lost in Maths, start by practising the part (a) questions in your past exam papers and work your way upwards to part (b) and so on.

Maths is about having a go, knowing the tricks, when to use formulae, consistent practice and really believing in your ability and the work you have done. For the rest of this chapter, I will look at seven key areas that will help you smash your target in this sometimes difficult subject:

Key Area One: Parents - You Need to Gently Introduce Maths Early Key Area Two: Thirty Top Tips for Excelling at Maths!

Key Area Three: Importance of Practising Exam Questions in Maths Key Area Four: Dealing with a Leaving Cert Maths Paper

Key Area Five: Time Management in Maths Key Area Six: The Language of Maths

Key Area Seven: Observational Trends in Maths

Key Area One: Parents - You Need to Gently Introduce Maths Early

Parents, I would advise you not to stand idly by in relation to Maths; you can't afford to. You may or may not have had a good experience in your own school days with Maths, but you need to leave that to one side now and get stuck in, as "you can help!" It is important to introduce Maths to your child from an early age so that they carry good habits with them into their teenage years. Maths appears in so many different tasks we do during our day; we are performing Maths calculations constantly and aren't even aware of it.

Young children are like sponges who love soaking up new information and experiences, so there are always opportunities to pass on lifelong skills to them in this subject. By involving them centrally in some of the activities and experiences listed below, you can turn them into amazing future Mathematicians and infuse a love for the subject, without them even knowing. As time passes, they will hopefully view Maths as a fun and challenging subject. The word Maths isn't mentioned once in the below list, but it is intrinsically linked to them all. Many of them can be reinforced up to early teenage years. Try opening discussions and involving them in the following day-to-day tasks:

- ♣ Setting the table for four people.

- ♣ Wrapping presents.

- ♣ Sorting and matching socks.

- ♣ Thinking about quantities and percentages in recipes.

- ♣ Reading the labels on food products.

- ♣ Organising notes and magnets on the fridge.

- ♣ Spotting shapes in the kitchen/garden.

♣ Adding up number plates when travelling.

♣ Listing where basic shapes exist: rectangle, triangle etc.

♣ Spotting shapes in books.

♣ Introducing days of the week.

♣ Introducing time of the day and minutes in a day.

♣ Introducing hours in the day and week.

♣ Introducing months and days in the year.

♣ Introducing yesterday, today, tomorrow, next week.

♣ Clocking numbers on cars, buses, shops, and houses.

♣ Measuring your child's height and discussing sizes.

♣ Converting their shoe size measurements i.e. between mm / cm.

♣ Regularly using the 'measure' words: tall, short, wide, narrow etc.

♣ laying counting games: Bingo, Snakes and Ladders and Dice.

♣ Making shapes with pasta, crayons, cut-outs.

♣ Showing them how to use a little ruler.

♣ Setting them little calculation challenges with rewards.

♣ Playing shop with kitchen products and money.

♣ Buying them a toy cash register.

♣ Using full and empty containers to introduce volume in baking.

♣ Comparing toys under size, weight, and shape.

♣ Making patterns with buttons or clothes pegs.

♣ Quizzing them on shapes around the home.

- ♣ Allowing them to scan the barcodes at the supermarket.

- ♣ Teaching them to divide treats evenly with their friends.

- ♣ Asking them to colour in bar charts and graphs.

- ♣ Showing them labels on food.

- ♣ Grouping clothes buttons together under size and shape.

- ♣ Giving them measuring tapes, rulers, watches, jugs, and scales.

- ♣ Challenging them to add and subtract basic numbers.

- ♣ Helping them to work out the change when you buy something.

- ♣ Downloading simple Maths games and apps for their tablets.

- ♣ Using food products to teach them about various shapes.

- ♣ Cutting paper to show how new shapes emerge from original ones.

- ♣ Setting them little number challenges with rewards.

- ♣ Discussing about the chance (probability) of an event happening.

Key Area Two: Thirty Top Tips for Excelling at Maths!

1. Learn the keywords from the official exam papers associated with each topic. Put formulas, explanation of words and keynotes into a little pocket notebook. Learn. (See Key Area Six below).

2. Practice as many past exam questions as you can and check your answers against fully developed and explained solutions.

3. Challenge yourself to try and come up with a second method of doing a specific question.

4. Try to approach each question from different angles. Always write down something. Do not be afraid of making a mistake.

5. Draw a diagram (if possible) and label it to simplify a question.

6. Be familiar with what is and what is not in your log tables.

7. When studying, exhaust all attempts to answer an exam question before referring to your solutions book. Do not give up easily.

8. Read each question in Maths carefully and underline or highlight the key words and phrases.

9. If you feel overwhelmed by the length and difficulty of the course – start with basic Algebra.

10. Find yourself a study buddy to share questions and resources with as well as, discuss problems and encourage each other.

11. Use various Internet sites as a companion to improve your Maths skills.

12. Consult your teacher about problems with topics or specific Maths questions during and after class. Download some Maths apps.

13. Start by attempting basic questions for each topic, building up to a full exam question. Answer the exact question being asked.

14. When completing a Maths question, do not skip any steps.

15. Do not be afraid to explain a solution to a question with words if you cannot do so with numbers and symbols.

16. Spend five to ten minutes going over what your teacher has done with you in class that day.

17. Every time you write down a formula, draw a box around it to help you remember it. Check if this formula is in your log tables. If not, you need to memorise it.

18. Anything that you type into your calculator (related to a question) must be written on your answer book also.

19. Have all resources present when doing Maths questions i.e. Full Maths set, pencil, calculator and log tables.

20. If you are a third or a sixth-year student, practice as many previous exam questions as you possibly can.

21. If Maths is a subject you struggle with, attempt this homework first when you are at your freshest.

22. Read a Maths question line by line, trying to understand what each line says before moving to the next one.

23. Give your teacher/the examiner plenty to correct in an exam, there are no marks for blanks.

24. Feel free to write on the question paper (especially if given a diagram) to gain a better understanding of the question.

25. Get familiar with all the buttons on your calculator especially the ones using second function (shift) button.

26. Always check back on your exam paper at the end of the exam to ensure you haven't made a basic calculation error. The same principle applies to homework.

27. All your friends are in the same boat. Believe in yourself.

28. You can only gain marks in Maths.

29. Try and approach Maths as a challenge not a task.

30. Buy a top-quality Exam Paper Solutions Book (Junior and Leaving Cert). i.e.

    See http://www.acesolutionbooks.com.

Key Area Three: Importance of Practising Exam Questions in Maths

Practising past exam questions is essential if you're looking to score highly in Maths. Similar question types come up over and over again, but you still need to revise all the topics on your course, as the Maths exam now is NOT predictable anymore. Both sections of the paper are equally important and sufficient time must be left for the longer questions as they tend to require more thought. Doing an exam question trial at home every week will improve your speed and accuracy for the Leaving Cert, and after some time you will cut out silly errors and feel calmer about tackling a full paper. This process will give you the belief that you can get the awkward question started and tackle the unseen diagram. The following is my reasoning to get quickly onto to the 'exam question' diet:

- ♣ You need to get practicing multiple real life application questions.

- ♣ You need to get familiar with the marking scheme.

- ♣ You need to practice exam questions under time pressure.

- ♣ You must constantly strive to get used to the wording, layout, and style of past exam questions.

- ♣ You need to get accustomed to how the examiners are phrasing the questions on the exam papers now.

- ♣ You need to be conscious of the fact that there is extra text and less numbers on the exam papers now.

- ♣ You need to be aware that you now could be asked to explain your answer.

- ♣ You need to be conscious of the possibility of being asked to 'give a reason for something' as opposed to 'stating facts'.

- ♣ You need to practise question types that ask if you agree with an opinion and why?

♣ You need to be aware that there is no choice on any of the papers.

♣ Through practice, you need to get used to coming up with a strategy to start unseen/unexpected questions.

♣ If English is a problem for you, Maths could now be a problem; so you need to be very familiar with the words that have come up on previous Maths papers. If you do not understand the meaning of a word, be sure to ask your teacher (See Key Area Six for extra information on this).

Key Area Four: Dealing with a Leaving Cert Maths Paper

No matter how intelligent you are or how well you prepare, if you are not exam smart, you will underachieve in Maths. It is vital to have a plan in place for each paper and be tactically aware, in case things go wrong in the exam. The following are my ACE tips to more efficiently deal with your Leaving Cert Maths paper:

♣ Units matter. If they are present in your question, they are required in your answer.

♣ As a rule of thumb, do not put anything into the calculator that you have not already written on your paper.

♣ You can get almost full marks (High partial credit) with just one slip/ mistake in your question. High partial credit could even be seven marks out of ten. Have a look at an example of a past paper marking scheme online for more details on credits.

♣ You must show your workings for all questions.

♣ If you make two or three attempts at a question, they will all be corrected and the highest marks from your efforts will be counted.

♣ Marks will be allocated for all work done on a diagram that has been printed on your exam paper.

♣ Be careful when dealing with minus signs.

♣ Write down every single step until you arrive at the solution.

♣ If your answer is 'off the wall', it is probably incorrect.

♣ If there are many steps required in a solution, you need to keep going back and checking completed steps for accuracy; otherwise you may need to re-write the whole solution again.

♣ Never rub/tippex out any work done even if you think it isn't neat. Draw a single line through the information as it will be corrected by the examiner later.

♣ When asked for your opinion, give it, and include some numbers (in the context of the question) with your answer if you can.

♣ Algebra is the bedrock of all Maths courses and is the main area that students struggle with. Practice it (big time).

♣ Practice questions involving real life statistics.

♣ Measuring and estimating the heights of objects outside is now an important part of Geometry and Trigonometry.

♣ In Co-ordinate Geometry, the slope of a line has become more important especially with respect to its context in a question.

♣ More recent Maths questions tend to contain more English, as more words are now required to describe real life situations. You need to be able to separate the important keywords in the text from the padding that surrounds them.

♣ Look through the wording of each question and pick out the Maths related information. In all subjects, but especially Maths, highlight the relevant pieces of the question with a highlighter. Watch out for numbers written as words, for example "thirty" instead of "30".

♣ If no diagram is drawn for you, try to draw one yourself to give a clearer picture of what is being asked. Mark in the given numerical information onto the diagram, ensuring it matches the text in the question.

♣ Do not leave any blanks ensuring that every question is fully attempted. If you leave a blank, the examiner will have no choice but to give you zero marks for that question part. If you attempt the question; you may get some marks and perhaps more than you think. In summary: No attempt = No marks.

♣ Know the theory and equations required for Trigonometry. If you are dealing with a Trigonometric problem know how to apply the three basic Trigonometric ratios; Pythagoras theorem, the sine rule, and the cosine rule. In these, you have all you need to solve a right-angled or a non-right-angled triangle problem.

♣ Relate the information you have in the exam question to the theory and equations you have worked on in class. In Geometry, have you got a right-angled triangle or a non-right-angled triangle? Have you got two right-angled triangles that need to be solved separately? Again, if you are unable to start a question, there is nearly always something you have learned from your teacher that you can draw on to help you.

♣ The relationship between two sets of data is important. This concept links up the slope of a line in Co-ordinate Geometry to that of correlation in Statistics. Other examples of where topics overlap in Maths include: Co-ordinate Geometry of the line and the Circle and of course Geometry and Trigonometry. There are many links between topics on the course now, so be sure to ask your teacher to help you understand them so that you are familiar with them before the exam.

Most importantly, remember that you are not alone and there are tens of thousands of other students in the same position as you on the day, many of them having had their struggles with Maths. If you are familiar with the main equations and some theory, you should have everything you need to attempt the paper and really give it your best shot.

Key Area Five: Time Management in Maths

...is crucial to exam success.

Allocate your time according to the amount of marks available for the question part. It will not be on the paper how many marks each specific part of a question will be worth and they tend to vary greatly. As with all subjects, make sure and be clear on the time allocation for each full question and move quickly and efficiently.

Questions are often split into parts (a), (b) and (c) etc. There is no fixed allocation of marks across these parts, but usually part (a) is the least difficult and part (c) or later is the most difficult; therefore, you may need more time for later parts. Try to pick up full marks on the easier parts and as many marks as you can on the rest, attempting every question part. Use the maximum time available to you by working right until the end of the exam.

In Maths, it is often a good idea to begin with your strongest question so as to extract as many marks as possible from it. Proceed with your second favourite, then third etc. I am not in favour of leaving all the long questions until last, due to the large amount of marks they carry. Make sure not to go over your calculated time on questions, as ultimately you will pay the price later in the exam. In Leaving Cert Maths, divide the amount of marks by two to work out how much time to spend on each question. At Junior Cycle level, the time recommended for each full question will be written at the top.

As with all subjects, but especially ones you find difficult, be ruthless with your time in the exam hall.

Key Area Six: The Language of Maths

In Maths, you must have a good solid Algebra foundation to build on in order to be able to attempt topics such as Calculus and Probability. Take time to understand all the rules of Algebra including those linked to expressions, functions, and graphs. Algebra is the most important topic in Maths but the language of Maths is equally important - the words and phrases that appear on the course and in your exam papers. The SEC now place more emphasis on students knowing and understanding what things mean in Maths than just being able to do numerical calculations. There are more words than ever on the Junior and Leaving Cert Maths exam papers and it is crucial that you start familiarising yourself with them.

If you are not familiar with the words and phrases that appear on the paper, you may not even be able to get a question started. This would be an awful shame given the amount of time you have spent learning mathematical concepts on your course. If you have dyslexia, I understand that dealing with words in Maths is doubly difficult. You need to be aware that different words have a different meaning, depending on the subject you are studying. For example, the word 'Evaluate' in Maths is very different to its meaning in English.

Table 2 below presents one hundred sample key words and phrases to kick start your understanding of the language of Maths. This list is suitable for both Junior and Senior Cycle, remembering that some of the more difficult words would not appear on a Junior Cycle paper. I would encourage you to add to my sample list below and investigate the exact meaning of the words that you discover; you will learn loads through your own investigations – learning by doing. As stated earlier, any time you come across a new Maths word or formula, write down what it means to you in an A5/ A6 notebook. This idea can be applied to all subjects and these notebooks can be carried with you all the way up to sixth year. Using simple explanations that you understand in your notebooks will help you recall what the words mean later. The following is a starter table containing key words and phrases (in alphabetical order) regularly seen on Maths exam papers:

Table 2: Sample Table of Maths Keywords and Phrases

	Keyword/ Phrase	Explanation
1.	**Acute**	The measure of this angle is between zero and ninety degrees.
2.	**Algorithm**	A step by step approach to solving a problem.
3.	**Analyse**	Identify relationships between parts, interpret and reach conclusions.
4.	**Apply**	Use the information given in the question to put forward a view point or give a real-life example.
5.	**Array**	An arrangement of numbers in row(s) and column(s).
6.	**Axis of Symmetry**	A line drawn through a shape that divides it perfectly in two. i.e. One side is the mirror image of the other.
7.	**Bar-Line Graph**	A graph containing vertical or horizontal lines that represents data (Similar to a Bar Chart except lines replace the Bars).
8.	**Bisector**	A line that divides another line, angle or shape into two equal parts.
9.	**Calculate**	Use your calculator to find the answer. The answer will be in numerical format.
10.	**Capacity**	The maximum volume of liquid/matter that a container can hold.
11.	**Cardinal Number**	The total amount of elements in a set. The symbol is #.
12.	**Central Symmetry**	Reflection of a point/line/shape through another point.

	Keyword/ Phrase	Explanation
13.	Circumference	The measured distance around the outside of a circle. (Same as Perimeter).
14.	Cluster	A tightly grouped set of numbers or data points.
15.	Comment	Give an opinion based on a given statement, result, calculation, or set of data values etc.
16.	Compare	Comment on the differences and similarities between two of more items/set of data values/opinions etc.
17.	Congruent Triangles	Two triangles that are identical in every way. i.e. equal angles and equal sides.
18.	Construct	This indicates creating/drawing something using a set square, protractor or ruler. Draw a diagram accurately e.g. One of the constructions on the course.
19.	Convert	Change the data given into another form.
20.	Correct to the nearest...	Round off your final answer into the units that are required in the question e.g. as a whole number or decimal places.
21.	Define	Write down the exact meaning of a word, phrase, or quantity.
22.	Denominator	The value on the bottom of a fraction.
23.	Derive	Arrive at a formula or statement by writing down a list of logical steps to get there OR change an existing Maths equation into a new one.
24.	Determine	Check if something is the case or not by using a series of Mathematical steps.
25.	Diameter	A line going from one side of a circle to the other through the centre. (Twice the Radius).

	Keyword/ Phrase	Explanation
26.	**Differentiate**	Find f'(x) or dy/dx for a given function OR Identify what makes something different.
27.	**Dividend**	An amount to be divided up into equal shares (parts).
28.	**Draw a Graph**	Use graph/grid paper to create an accurate labelled graph with a ruler.
29.	**Element**	Part of a set. e.g. Blue is an element of the colours. The Symbol is ε.
30.	**Equation**	A Mathematical expression with variables/numbers and an equals. e.g. 2x+4=10.
31.	**Equivalent**	The same as. (Similar to 'Equals').
32.	**Estimate**	Make an approximate guess to the best of your ability without using your calculator.
33.	**Evaluate**	Find the 'value' using your calculator. This normally requires replacing (subbing in) a letter with a number. e.g. replace x with 3 when told 'x = 3'.
34.	**Exponential**	Power. e.g. 3^4 (Where 4 is the exponent-Similar to 'Index').
35.	**Express**	Put one number over another and find a % OR Express 16 in the form of 2^x i.e. Ans: 2^4
36.	**Factor**	A number that divides evenly into another number (1 is always a factor).
37.	**Factorise**	Write down the factors of …Usually using brackets.
38.	**Find**	Using the information and/or diagram given to write down the answer required.
39.	**Frequency**	How often an event occurs.

	Keyword/ Phrase	Explanation
40.	Give your answer in the form of...	Write your final answer in the specific format requested in the question... e.g. a+bi for a complex number question.
41.	Graph	Draw a neat graph on grid/graph paper with a ruler or a draw a freehand curve.
42.	Hence	Use the last answer from the previous question. Copy down the previous answer and continue.
43.	Identify	Recognise patterns, facts OR pick out an answer from a list OR State a unique fact or feature of something.
44.	Improper Fraction	A fraction where the numerator (top number) is greater than the denominator (bottom number).
45.	Integer	Minus and plus whole numbers. i.e. -2,-1,0,1,2...
46.	Interpret	Use knowledge and understanding to recognise trends and draw conclusions from them.
47.	Intersection	What two data sets have in common. i.e. The bit in the middle where they meet.
48.	Investigate	Check/Test if something occurs or not. It may OR may not be true. Reach some conclusion.
49.	...in the Domain	May appear in a graphing question: Draw your graph using values between two numbers listed. e.g.: -1 > x > 4. In this case, use -1, 0, 1, 2, 3, 4 for the x values on your graph. Find y values and draw.
50.	Justify	Give sound reasons with supporting evidence for providing an answer.
51.	List	Write down numbers/letters in a line, separated by a comma.
52.	Magnitude	The measure of the size of an object.

	Keyword/ Phrase	Explanation
53.	Mean	The average of a set of values. i.e. Add them up and divide by the amount of values.
54.	Measure	Physically use a measuring tool e.g. A ruler.
55.	Median	The middle number when the numbers are listed in ascending order.
56.	Mode	The value that appears most often on a list.
57.	Multiple	Obtained by multiplying the number by any other number. e.g. multiples of 5 are 5,10,15, 20 etc. (Similar to times tables).
58.	Name	Write down the letters on a shape/angle in the order they appear on it. e.g. Triangle abd.
59.	Natural Number	A positive whole number. i.e. 1,2,3,4...
60.	Net	The development of an object when laid out flat.
61.	Null Set	A set with nothing in it. e.g. The amount of males in an all-female room.
62.	Numerator	The value on the top of a fraction.
63.	Obtuse Angle	The measure of this angle is between ninety and one hundred and eighty degrees.
64.	Order	Put values into a numerical list depending on how large they are (i.e. ascending or descending order).
65.	Perimeter	This is the measured distance around the outside of a shape. (Same as Circumference for a circle).
66.	Perpendicular Bisector	A line that divides another line in two and is at ninety degrees to it.
67.	Perpendicular Line	A line that makes a ninety degree angle with another line.

	Keyword/ Phrase	Explanation
68.	Plot	This refers to putting co-ordinates (x,y) on an Argand diagram for a 'Complex Numbers' question OR Plotting the values of X and Y on a co-ordinate diagram to draw a graph.
69.	Predict	The expected future values of a data set given what you know of the existing trend.
70.	Prism	A uniform shape with two polygons (2d shape) connected by a series of parallel lines.
71.	Product	The answer when two terms or numbers are multiplied.
72.	Prove	Referring to 'Prove a theorem' in Geometry. The steps of 'proof' must be written down in a logical order. (Similar to 'Show' and 'Verify', the statement must be true).
73.	Quadrilateral	A four sided figure.
74.	Quotient	A fraction.
75.	Range	The difference (subtract) between the maximum and the minimum value.
76.	Reflex Angle	The measure of this angle is between one hundred and eighty and three hundred and sixty degrees.
77.	Represent	Create or Fill in a diagram as required. e.g. A Venn diagram in sets.
78.	Right Angle	Ninety degree angle.
79.	Rounding	Write down the nearest rounded figure to a specific number. It may involve decimal places. e.g. Rounding off to two decimal places.
80.	Sample Space	A list of the total possible outcomes of an experiment or trial.
81.	Shade	Highlight the region or area with your pencil that is being requested.
82.	Show	Prove that something occurs. (Similar to 'Prove' and 'Verify', it must be true).

	Keyword/ Phrase	Explanation
83.	Similar Triangles	Two triangles that have equal angles.
84.	Simplest form	Break down your answer as much as you can. May involve dividing it by a number to reduce it.
85.	Simplify	Make easier by multiplying out the brackets OR converting two fractions into one etc.
86.	Sketch	Make a quick but neat drawing of a diagram, picture, image or graph on your page.
87.	Solution Set	Write the final answer in the format of a set (with curly brackets) after you reach the solution to the question.
88.	Solve	Find 'x' or 'y' or both. In Algebra terms, it means 'find the root(s)'.
89.	Square Number	The result you get when you multiply a number by itself. 1(1x1), 4(2x2), 9(3x3) etc.
90.	State	Provide a short statement on a topic.
91.	Subset	Part of a set. e.g. Yellow is a subset of the colours.
92.	Suggest	Propose a solution or answer to a question asked.
93.	Sum	Add up the terms in the question.
94.	Tessellation	A repeating pattern that fits perfectly together.
95.	Use the Graph to...	Read a value off your graph as requested. A ruler might be helpful here. Make sure and show workings on your graph.

	Keyword/ Phrase	Explanation
96.	**Variable**	A letter that can represent a number in an equation. e.g. the letter 'y' in 2y+5=9
97.	**Verify**	Check your answer by substituting back a number into the original equation/formula. It should always sub in perfectly. A statement you are asked to 'Verify' is always true. (Similar to 'Show' and 'Prove').
98.	**Vertex**	One of the corner points of a triangle. (Plural: Vertices).
99.	**Whole Numbers**	Numbers that do not contain decimals. All Integers.
	Write an Expression	Write down a term/set of terms with letters and numbers in it. e.g. $n^2 + 2$.

Key Area Seven: Observational Trends in Maths

I think both you and your parents need to be aware of the following observations in relation to gender that has emerged since the inception of Project Maths (Incidentally 'Project Maths' was the name used to rebrand Maths) in 2008.

Firstly, in general, I have noticed that some of my students (and those of my colleagues) are experiencing a slight dip in Maths results during their second year in school, due to the increased workload and other external factors. The dip for girls is not as pronounced as for boys. There is also a dip in fifth year but it isn't as extreme as the second year one. If your child is in second year, you need to be aware that this could be the case for them. I believe that working on their Algebra skills is a big factor in combatting this problem as it underpins many questions especially at higher level.

Secondly, from the students I have taught since Project Maths was introduced, I have noticed another trend in my classes. I have spotted that girls are less likely to take risks when answering exam questions. The new phrasing of questions on Maths papers suit boys better as they are less conscious of what they are writing down and are less afraid of being wrong. In my opinion, it is important for girls to be able to express their opinions freely and openly and we, as teachers, need to help them develop this skill. Courage will grow by taking risks. I think it is important for all students not to get overly upset if they cannot get a certain part of a question out perfectly. It is more important to keep going with the paper, instead of looking to complete every single question part absolutely perfect. One doesn't really have time for this on a Maths paper as they tend to be quite long and unlike other subjects there isn't as much time for contemplation of excellence.

Thirdly, girls especially need to practice more exam questions involving engineering and mechanical parts. My reasoning for this is that in general, most of the student cohort studying Engineering, Construction studies and Design/Communication Graphics (DCG) at Leaving Cert level are boys, and girls are not being exposed to this specific type of learning. With more everyday life questions being the order of the day in Maths, it is inevitable that more technical and mechanical questions will appear in years to come, and girls and parents of girls need to be aware of this. This trend will slowly become more pronounced if the Governments' promotion and focus on the Science, Technology, Engineering and Maths (STEM) subjects continues and I expect it will.

Lastly, in a recent survey, twenty-nine percent of Irish parents surveyed thought that technology subjects weren't suitable for girls and fifty-three percent of girls in secondary school dropped STEM subjects due to pressure from their parents. These statistics may be contributing to the lack of representation of females working in STEM fields. Students and parents need to be aware of the excellent third level courses and future career opportunities available in these areas, no matter what a person's gender is. Students need to be encouraged to explore all avenues of interest and follow their career path of choice.

Naturally, being aware of current developments and up to date trends in subjects is useful when you are preparing to sit an exam or pursue a possible career in them.

ACE Inspirational Quotes

"The laws of nature are but the mathematical thoughts of God"
Euclid.

"Mathematics is one of the essential emanations of the human spirit, a thing to be valued in and for itself, like art or poetry"
Oswald Veblen.

Chapter 9:

Significant Advice from Students

This book, so far, is based on my research, advice, and experience along with knowledge from my teaching colleagues. You are all familiar with teachers advising you about subjects and decisions; I'd be pretty sure that some of the content of this book has been repeated by your teachers in class. I know also that many of you would like to hear your fellow students' perspective, especially those who have completed their exams. It is a long time since I sat in an exam hall, so I wanted to have a chapter where student opinions were aired and feedback was relevant. This chapter will give you a sense of the reality and the pressures of the current Leaving Certificate exam from a student's perspective.

I have listened carefully and recorded information from students who have been through both the Junior and Leaving Cert exams over many years. I have also surveyed sixty existing sixth years for their first-hand experience, asking them to think back to how they were feeling and their approach to the Junior Cycle exams; what they did right, what they could have done better, big mistakes and importantly what they learned.

To finish, I publish two excellent unedited passages honestly written by recent Leaving Cert students who detail their success story and give loads of brilliant guidance. Again, I have opted for a bullet point format in this chapter; making it easier for you to read and understand. It is straight to the (bullet) point; literally. The students have touched on many interesting and relevant points, along with some surprising results arising from my survey. The information gathered from the students is broken up into five main areas:

1. The Importance of Homework

2. Preparing Properly Through Fifth and Sixth Year

3. Students' Big, Big Tips for Achieving Success

4. "Being Exam Smart"- Survey of Leaving Certificate Students

5. "Everything Will Work Out in The End"– A Tale of Two Emily's

1. The Importance of Homework

Firstly, I asked students to think about the importance of homework to them and how its benefits helped them achieve their goals. Here are some of the observations they made about it:

♣ Record your homework carefully in your journal every day.

♣ Use class time well if teachers allot it to homework.

♣ Set the same time aside every evening for homework.

♣ Do your homework after dinner and soon after arriving home.

♣ Try to complete the majority of homework before nine p.m.

♣ Try to be honest with your teachers in relation to homework.

♣ Tick off your homework for each subject as it gets done.

♣ When doing your homework, don't lounge on a bed or sofa.

♣ Ask your parents/teacher if you can't understand your homework.

♣ Have a quiet study area with a desk, fresh air, and good lighting.

♣ As well as written work, browse over what was covered in class.

♣ Don't let homework affect sleep time.

♣ Plan ahead on assignments if you are expecting a busy week.

♣ Get the phone numbers of classmates for queries on homework.

♣ Leaving homework until the next morning is a bad idea.

2. Preparing Properly Through Fifth and Sixth Year

I then asked the students to provide some study guidance for current Fifth and Sixth years. Here is a summary of what they said about preparing properly in order to maximise learning during the two years of Senior Cycle:

♣ Start studying now.

♣ Everything happens for a reason.

♣ Start practising exam questions.

♣ Do practice exams at home under exam conditions.

♣ Separate notes with labelled dividers to make topics easier to find.

♣ As you approach exams, continue to attend class to the end.

♣ Rest up well during the spring mid-term break.

♣ Go hard up until your mocks and take a break after them, returning to a consistent routine afterwards.

♣ Failure to plan is planning to fail. Plan each day using your homework journal.

♣ Once an exam is done, take a break, move on, and start thinking about the next exam, never look back.

♣ Homework, revision and creating good quality notes are all forms of study.

♣ Breaking a topic into bullet points is a brilliant way to help you remember it.

♣ Get into a routine of study, exercise, social life etc., i.e. Every Monday; do the same thing, same on Tuesday etc. Stick to this consistently and you will be able to plan ahead better.

♣ Do extra study in the part of the day you feel more alert depending on whether you're a night owl or an early bird (This only applies to weekends and holiday periods obviously).

♣ Try and do a similar amount of study every week so that your mind and body gets used to it. Too much in one session can leave you tired and too little is obviously not enough.

♣ Exercise will keep your mind fresh. Walking, gym sessions, cycling, swimming, or Zumba classes are all good. Do something you enjoy, whatever that may be.

♣ If you happen to be over eighteen, minimise the consumption of alcohol in sixth year. It will affect your concentration and work during the following few days. If you wish to, you can have plenty of nights out during the summer. Abstaining will ensure you feel better in yourself and get more done in your final year.

♣ It may not be your favourite year in school due to the pressure and amount of work your teachers will expect of you. However, sixth year is just one year of hard work. It will all be worth it in the end and you will be proud of yourself on results day for the effort you have put in.

♣ From the month of March onwards in sixth year, you need to be punching in at least four hours of work per night. For example, five thirty p.m. to ten p.m. This includes homework and short breaks.

♣ You need to figure out how best you learn. Some students learn by writing things out repeatedly, some by talking it out in groups, some by listening to recordings, some by reading, some by Internet research and others by typing out keynotes. A combination of the above learning styles may be your key to success.

♣ Try not to approach the Leaving Cert with a negative frame of mind. If you constantly think 'I have to do so much study', it will be like carrying around a bag of coal. If you don't like a subject, think 'This subject isn't my favourite' as opposed to 'I hate this subject'. Thinking about life more positively can help you approach problem solving better.

♣ Get yourself a study buddy for the subjects you find difficult. You can work together on questions, share information, and encourage each other to make the subject more understandable. It is also a great way to get organised and relieve some tension.

♣ Share work around in a small group. Have information sharing sessions in someone's house. This reduces the amount of preparation you need to do in each subject, as your friends will already have done the research and checks on it. Sit down with the group and explain things to each other. Write down the key points from the shared session to enhance your own set of notes.

♣ Prior to the exams (the last six weeks), do some morning trial runs on food. You will definitely need to eat something for breakfast on the days you are doing exams.

♣ The mock exams are a good time to trial new foods and good habits in preparation for the Leaving Cert. You should discover which foods help you feel good and give you more energy.

♣ Know your exam paper well. Know the exact date and time the paper is on. Know how long it is. Know how many questions you need to complete. Know how many marks are available for each question.

♣ Be ruthless with your time. Allocate a time limit for each part of a question (depending on the marks available for that part).

♣ Social media and mock papers only speculate about the contents of the final exam papers. Nobody really has a clue what's on the paper, despite what they may say or have read online.

♣ Believe in yourself. You have come so far and have so many talents that cannot be measured by any final exam. Your results in this exam will not affect how proud your parents are of you or how important you are to all your friends.

♣ Start studying now (again!).

3. Students' Big, Big Tips for Achieving Success

On asking students for one piece of advice that they would give to sixth years doing exams, these are the best 'one liners' they came up with:

♣ Try not to bottle exam stress up. Talk to your friends and parents.

♣ Don't beat yourself up when you are not studying.

♣ Try to keep sleep, eating, and studying patterns consistent.

♣ Understanding words is better than memorising them.

♣ Play some loud music or head out dancing every so often.

♣ Stop and count to ten if you feel anxious.

♣ Use your own words when taking notes. Keep the notes short.

♣ Breathe deeply into your lungs to help combat nerves.

♣ Exercise to help reduce tension.

♣ Your parents can be a great source of advice.

♣ Speak to your teachers all the way up to exam start.

♣ Stay away from stressed out friends for a few weeks.

♣ Keep eating proper breakfasts and dinners.

♣ Underline the key words on the exam paper to focus your mind.

♣ Bring earplugs into the exam hall to help your concentration.

♣ Get into some good study habits at the beginning of third year.

♣ Start creating a weekly timetable to help you study in third year.

♣ Pay attention to all your subjects, not just the ones you like.

♣ Don't isolate yourself from your friends in third year.

♣ Continue the hobbies you enjoy during exam year.

♣ Don't expect too much of yourself.

♣ Ask your teachers loads of questions. They love that.

♣ Your teachers have every confidence and belief in you.

♣ Don't believe everything your peers say online.

♣ Try not to pressure yourself, you are probably ready anyway.

♣ Take a step back from social media around exam time.

♣ Treat yourself to good breaks when you are studying.

♣ Your friends will also be nervous on day one of the exams.

♣ Doing your homework well is the best form of study.

♣ Go out with your friends to chill at some stage during the exams.

♣ Be super organised, especially the week leading up to the exams.

♣ Plan each study day in between exams.

♣ Go for walks or cycles to get fresh air around exam time.

♣ Stick post-its/posters up in your room to help memory.

♣ Practice as many past exam questions as you have time to do.

♣ Always remember your parents/relations are very proud of you.

♣ Buy a good solutions book for subjects you find difficult.

♣ Work hard and play a little during the few weeks of the exams.

♣ Double check all your materials are present the night before.

♣ Accept that not everything will go exactly to plan.

♣ Work with your friends on subjects you are struggling with.

♣ Try and enjoy the challenge of preparing for exams.

♣ Do every piece of homework as if it was an exam question.

♣ Be sure to ask your teacher if you don't understand something.

♣ Focus heavily on exam questions the week before the exams.

♣ Use varied methods of studying to avoid boredom.

♣ Keep a copy of your exam timetable in your room.

♣ If an exam doesn't go so well, move on, focus on the next one.

♣ Reward yourself with little food treats around exam time.

♣ Use the Internet to look up information that's not in your book.

♣ Re-write notes in your own words so that you understand them.

♣ Stay positive.

♣ Write down a vision for your life.

♣ Always see can you improve what you are doing.

♣ Occasionally do something nice for other people.

♣ Set goals to ensure you are still moving in the right direction.

♣ Ask your friends about the different ways they study.

♣ Be aware of time spent on the Internet and phone.

♣ Be careful who you share your dreams with.

♣ Ask yourself "Am I going in the right direction?"

♣ Record on a sheet all the good things in your life.

♣ During exam year, try and block out the negatives.

♣ Record all your thoughts of the day on a sheet; then shred it.

♣ Focus on the positives.

♣ If you keep doing the same thing, nothing will change.

♣ Write a to-do list crossing items out when achieved.

♣ While studying, turn off the mobile phone and close your e-mail.

♣ Think you can do it, know you can do it, do it and be persistent.

♣ When studying, do the hardest thing first.

♣ Keep a tidy desk and a clean bedroom.

♣ Have some type of study timetable in place.

4."Being Exam Smart"- Survey of Leaving Certificate Students

In order to get more information about how students perceived exams completed, I decided to survey a small cohort of sixty existing Leaving Certificate students. In the survey, I asked them about attitudes to exams, advice they would give to current students and also what would have been of benefit to them in their last big exam. I think many of the responses reinforce the points I have made throughout this book, although there are some interesting and surprising ones in there. In reading the responses, I hope that you will recognise your own situation in many of them. A number 'one' response denotes the most popular option the students wrote down, with number ten being the least popular. A copy of the survey is available to view in the Appendix.

The following are the exact results of the survey:

When asked: **"What are the important things to do around exam time?"** The following were the top ten responses in order of popularity:

Table 3: What are the important things to do around exam time?

Order	Student Response
1	Study
2	Sleep well
3	Rest, relax and breaks
4	Eat well
5	Stay calm
6	Drink plenty of water
7	Practice past exam questions
8	Get prepared
9	Revise
10	Make time for friends

When asked: **"What are important things not to do around exam time?"** The following were the top ten responses in order of popularity:

Table 4: What are important things not to do around exam time?

Order	Student Response
1	Not get stressed out
2	Not get enough sleep
3	Stay up too late studying
4	Stay out partying all night
5	Eat poorly
6	Not planning your revision
7	Study without breaks
8	Not exercise
9	Be on social media and phone constantly
10	Not stick to a study timetable

When asked: **"How are you going to go about studying as the exams near?"**
The following were the top ten responses in order of popularity:

Table 5: How are you going to go about studying as the exams near?

Order	Student Response
1	Practice past exam style questions
2	Create flash cards
3	Create a plan
4	Follow a study timetable
5	Write out my own set of notes
6	Stay calm and relaxed
7	Take breaks
8	Sleep well
9	Prioritise more difficult subjects
10	Get help from my friends

When asked: **"What advice would you give to third year students?"** The following were the top ten responses in order of popularity:

Table 6: What advice would you give to third year students?

Order	Student Response
1	Don't stress
2	Study, but take time out
3	Don't worry, be happy
4	Revise a small bit every night
5	Practice past exam questions
6	Make a realistic study plan
7	Revise topics from second year
8	There is more to life than exams
9	Concentrate in class
10	Enjoy it

When asked: **"If you could get hold of information from someone to advise you about exams, what information would be helpful to you?"** The following were the top ten responses in order of popularity:

Table 7: If you could get hold of information from someone to advise you about exams, what information would be helpful to you?

Order	Student Response
1	Effective study techniques and tips
2	Examples of possible questions
3	Help with the wording of questions
4	A notes summary of topics covered
5	Information about how the marking schemes work
6	How to layout a good study plan
7	Information to help me manage my time
8	Dealing with the stress of doing the exams
9	How to organise myself and avoid distractions
10	How to begin studying different subjects

When asked: **"What parts of doing exams do you struggle with?"**
The following were the top ten responses in order of popularity:

Table 8: What parts of doing exams do you struggle with?

Order	Student Response
1	Getting the timing right
2	Stress and pressure of exams
3	Understanding the meaning of questions
4	Too much information to learn off
5	Staying focused
6	Trying to remember information I have learned
7	Concentration
8	Motivation
9	Fear of failure
10	Structuring my answers properly

When asked: **"What three pieces of advice would you give to younger students, i.e. First, second and third years doing class exams in May?"**
The following were the top ten responses in order of popularity:

Table 9: What three pieces of advice would you give younger students i.e. First, second and third years doing class exams in May?

Order	Student Response
1	Stay calm and don't stress
2	Do your best
3	Keep on top of your homework
4	Make a revision plan
5	Revise every night what you did in class
6	Eat well
7	Get plenty of sleep
8	Ask your teacher for help
9	Spend extra time on the subjects you struggle with
10	Pay attention in class

When asked: **"Name something that would have been really helpful before your last exam?"** The following were the top ten responses in order of popularity:

Table 10: Name something that would have been really helpful before your last exam?

Order	Student Response
1	Knowing how to manage my time well
2	Knowing ways to cope with stress
3	Extra tuition
4	Tips on how to study properly
5	Having a good study plan in place
6	Knowing how to structure answers well
7	Extra guidance from teachers
8	Tips to sleep better
9	More praise from teachers
10	A chat with my class mates to relieve stress

When asked: **"List some things you found important about homework?"**

The following were the top ten responses in order of popularity:

Table 11: List some things you found important about homework?

Order	Student Response
1	It's a great form of revision
2	It helps me remember things better
3	It helps me practice what I have learned
4	It helps me understand where I may need help
5	It keeps information fresh in my head
6	It tests if I was listening in class
7	It provides an honest assessment of my progress
8	It prepares me to do exam questions later
9	It works well if it is challenging
10	It sets a great base for later study

When asked: **"List seven tips you would give to someone preparing for exams?"** The following were the top ten responses in order of popularity:

Table 12: List seven tips you would give to someone preparing for exams?

Order	Student Response
1	Relax loads
2	Sleep plenty
3	Eat healthy food
4	Exercise
5	Take breaks
6	Stick with your study plan
7	Keep in touch with friends
8	Keep on top of homework
9	Study in short bursts
10	Stay off your social media/phone

When asked: **"What would you say to Junior Cycle students about how to handle the pressure and do the right thing in the exam hall?"** The following were the top ten responses in order of popularity:

Table 13: What would you say to Junior Cycle students about how to handle the pressure and do the right thing in the exam hall?

Order	Student Response
1	Stay calm and breathe
2	Be aware of your timing
3	Bring in water
4	Concentrate and focus on your paper
5	Don't be looking around you and getting distracted
6	Ignore what other students are doing
7	Imagine yourself working at home on your own
8	Check you have everything you need beforehand
9	Bring a top with you in case it is cold in there
10	Read each question properly

When asked: **"What mistakes did you feel you made just before the Junior Cycle exam and inside the exam hall on the day?** You can include issues in class or mock exams." The following were the top ten responses in order of popularity:

Table 14: What mistakes did you feel you made just before the Junior Cycle exam and inside the exam hall on the day? You can include issues in class or mock exams.

Order	Student Response
1	I didn't do enough work
2	I didn't read the questions properly
3	I was distracted looking at other students
4	I worried too much before the exams
5	I got the timing on the day wrong
6	I didn't prepare enough over the last three months
7	I crammed at the last minute
8	I was up late a few nights before exams
9	I didn't structure my answers well
10	I listened to other students' predictions

5."Everything Will Work Out in The End"– A Tale of Two Emily's

The following is a letter written by a recent Leaving Cert to all students sitting exams. Emily Bollard aced 577 points and is now studying Science at University College Dublin (UCD). From her experience, she offers insights, advice and recommendations for those getting ready for their exams:

Dear Leaving Certs,

Everyone has their own way of coping with the pressure of Leaving Cert year, and undoubtedly you will hear plenty of coping strategies during it. Teachers, parents, siblings, neighbours and anyone else who claim to have survived the "toughest exam you'll ever sit" will be lining up to advise you on the "best" way to approach your exams. Although they might know what's best for you (or think they do), the only person who truly knows whats best for you, is you. Here are a few generic tips and exam survival strategies:

Stay calm

This applies to every aspect of the Leaving Cert, from filling out your CAO application to the exam hall process. Always remember to relax! The mocks might be the first instance where you feel you won't be able to survive the year. This will be your first experience of working under exam-style conditions, so naturally enough; it's bound to be pretty daunting. Getting overly stressed in the exam hall will reduce your ability to retain information, that you have spent time studying. So sit back, close your eyes and take a deep breath. Tell yourself that "you can do it" and that "you know how to do it", and then take another look at the paper. If a question is still causing you trouble, simply skip it, revisiting it later.

Aim higher, achieve higher

Always aim for higher grades than is required for the course you want. Although this is easier said than done, it is essential due to the unpredictability of the points system. The more popular a course is, the more likely the points are to increase, so aim for one grade above what you need, based on last year's points. You will be surprised by what you're capable of achieving and indeed many of my friends were this year.

There's always another way

When someone tells you "Everything will work out in the end", it does actually turn out that way. If you are aiming for a Level eight course, don't rule out the possibility of doing a Level six/seven or a PLC one. Think about it- would you rather spend a year doing a PLC course and find out that's really what you want to do, or repeat the Leaving Cert? On your CAO form, choose courses you would enjoy or have a genuine interest in. Choosing your courses carefully, along with having a backup plan, will reduce the risk of having to repeat. Never mind what your parents want you to do and don't be put off by teachers' opinions of certain courses - choose the path that will bring you joy, not money. Keep your options open, looking at different routes to get where you want. If you really want something, you can achieve it. Remember-"Where there's a will, there's a way!"

Leave on a high note

In the midst of all the exam drama, we tend to forget the significance of sixth year-it's our final year in school! It's not all about studying; there should be an element of fun as you hang out with your classmates. Enjoy your final year and make as many new friends as you can, ensuring you'll leave with a precious collection of memories and emotions. Work hard, but don't put your life on hold totally for the exams. Finally, prepare well, enjoy every moment and most importantly, be happy. These should get you through the year in one piece! As Les Brown once said:

"Shoot for the moon. Even if you miss, you will land among the stars".

Best wishes for your future,

Emily Bollard.

The following is an article written by former Leaving Cert student Emily White who scored a credible 444 points in her exams. Emily has since been inspiring students by producing Leaving Cert YouTube videos with a combined rate of fifteen thousand hits and is now studying a Bachelor of Science in Psychology at Dublin City University (DCU).

My journey

Re-winding three years ago and I was in a panic over the fast approaching Leaving Cert exams. It was only September and I was already apprehensive of how they would go. I was putting so much pressure on myself needing to get "x" amount of points to get the course I wanted, otherwise I was a failure. It was only after I had sat all of my exams and started college that I realised how much hype surrounds the Leaving Cert. Three years down the track, I can barely remember my grades. However, I was there and I know its importance to you at this moment. I will reflect back now on how it was for me, which hopefully will help you in some way.

These are your exams

Firstly, it is important to be clear on one thing. You are sitting this exam for you and only you; I wish someone had told me this. We often get caught up in expectations from friends, family and even teachers and this adds to the pressure.

At the beginning of fifth year, choose subjects you love, ones you know you will thrive in. Picking the right ones are so important and if I had done this, I may have avoided the extra tutoring at lunch, to scrape a pass in a subject I didn't enjoy. During the year, do not compare your results in class tests to others, focusing more on improving your own result from previous exams rather than peer comparisons.

Organisation

A cliché, I know, but organisation is essential for doing well in your exams. Once settled into sixth year, put a study timetable routine in place. Regularly sit down and plan your study for the week ahead. Record how long it takes to revise a topic, as this will help you to optimise planning for revisiting this topic later in the year. Setting small achievable goals on a weekly basis is vital, as these will eventually build into your long term goal-the exams.

As the year progress, deadlines will arrive at you from all directions: listening exams, orals, class tests. One tactic I found useful was the idea of using 'pretend deadlines'. Let's say you have a language oral in a month's time; pretend it is actually in two weeks. That way, when the exam actually arrives, you will be more than prepared for it. It is hard, not to get overwhelmed during exam year, but prioritising important work can really help. Decide what needs to be done first, and then move to the next most important task. This worked well for me and there is honestly nothing more satisfying than ticking off a 'to do' list.

Balance

Balance throughout leaving cert year is critical to performing well. Schedule time for friends, family and exercise; as time away from the books will actually help your study long term and give you headspace. If someone is slicing a cake, the slices would normally be different sizes. Your leaving cert year needs to be balanced like that, ensuring that your 'studying slice' isn't way bigger than the others. Try not to fall into the trap of revising your favourite subject the most; as others get neglected then.

Balance also involves studying in different ways. For example in English, I recorded myself reading poems and then listened to them on the walk to school. I switched the language on my phone to French in order to incorporate it into my everyday life and in Biology; I drew out labelled diagrams and hung them up around my room. Try anything and everything that will help you remember is my advice.

Put yourself first

Whilst technology can be very beneficial for studying, it is also a massive distraction. Put your phone out of the room or give it to one of your parents, whilst you revise or do homework. Delete unnecessary apps, unfollow people that clog up your social media and question what benefits Facebook, Twitter and Instagram are providing for you. We spend hours aimlessly scrolling through social media, where instead we could be using this time to socialise in real life, play a sport or do some important revision.

In general, be clever in your studying habits, making sure you enjoy the year and spend loads of time with your friends. Looking back, a lifestyle balance and good organisation was what I found most helpful in my final year.

Good luck to all of you,

Emily White.

ACE Inspirational Quotes

———— ♥ ♠ ♦ ♣ ————

"Anyone who has never made a mistake
has never tried anything new"
Albert Einstein.

"Perfection is not attainable, but if we
chase perfection we can catch excellence"
Vince Lombardi.

Chapter 10:

Parenting an Exam Student

As a parent, I feel that you have a big responsibility around exam time. As you well know, you have had a big influence on your child's development over the last seventeen or so years and you are now encouraging them to reach their goals and take flight. Your children respect and look up to you; you are their most influential role model and the advice and positivity you give them around exam time is crucial. Consider your role as a valve on a tyre; trying to release the pressure on them as best you can. You need to expect that the media, their teachers and even their peers may add to your child's anxiety, whether intentional or not. Each child will deal with these pressures in their own way, it is only you that really knows your own child, so you will best know how to keep them calm and reassure them.

You will find loads of useful information dotted around various chapters in this book and I highly recommend a flick through the other nine chapters to get more of an understanding what your child is facing into. This chapter contains advice for you to better help your child navigate the education system successfully, and ultimately ACE their final exams.

Challenge Your Child with Education

You remember your child's primary school days particularly between third and sixth class, when you started to realise their potential and which subjects they would struggle with and excel in. Parents often ask me 'Is Maths something children are just naturally good at or is it something that can be learned?' From speaking to hundreds of parents over the years, some of you think that very little can be done if your child is struggling with a particular subject. I feel strongly that a potential mini crisis can be averted between the ages of eight and twelve in the way they are prepared for secondary school. Firstly, showing an interest in the child's work and progress in school between these ages greatly helps. Secondly, parents that use their inherent intelligence and life experience to teach their child the ways of the world greatly enhance the richness of learning for them. All parents already do this, but I feel it should be underpinned by stimulating and challenging the child Educationally.

Feeding Habits

It is important to set in motion good eating habits that will stand to your child for their future. In today's kitchen, there are issues with: food intolerances/allergies, conflicting information on nutrition, fussy kids, gluten free, coeliac, and most alarmingly, a rise in obesity. Conflicting information can lead to confusion over which foods are actually good for them. You need to keep up to date with which foods are wholesome for your child and pass on this information to them. Forgetting fads and trends, I prefer to just keep it simple in relation to nutrition.

Experts agree that we should endeavour to construct much of our diet from fruit and vegetables and that education on healthy eating must begin at home. An idea like putting a poster up in the kitchen, stating that we need to 'Eat The Rainbow' every week, could work in an effort to see how many different colours we can get onto their plate. We all know kids that are fussy eaters, but if they like only one out of the three vegetables we have introduced to them, this is success. It has to be said that we all ate what was put on the plate in front of us as a child, so I don't believe you should let your child dictate everything either. There is a balance to be struck here, exposing them to as many nutritious foods as possible. We've all heard the saying 'You are what you eat'. What we eat can affect our bodies, our mood, our memory, our handling of stress and our ability to complete simple daily tasks. This is escalated during times of intense mental stress, like exam time.

Having done a nice bit of research on nutrition myself; I would encourage you to expose your children to as wide a variety of foods as early as possible. Excellent foods with a sound nutritional value include: Turkey, Fish, Broccoli, Cauliflower, Walnuts, Almonds, Oats, Avocado, Grapefruit, Apple Cider Vinegar, Potatoes, Carrots, Tomatoes, Bananas, Blueberries, Raspberries, Lemons, Limes, Turmeric, Basmati Rice, Brown Rice, Puffed Spelt (Sugar puffs without the sugar), Cucumber, Beetroot, Spinach and of course, loads and loads of Water. On the face of it, this looks like a very aspirational list but you could start by gradually introducing three or four of them. I have felt the benefit of these types of foods over the years and maybe your family can too. Chapter Six: Exam Time=Feeding Time will provide you with plenty of advice around what your child should eat during the exams, with a focus on optimal nutrition for their three main meals.

Guidelines for Meal Routines

The most important thing is to strive for balance and endeavour to get your child into good eating habits. Nutrition is vital at any time of year, but especially during exam time when the brain and body are under particular stress. There is no need to cook separate meals or to spend a fortune on 'new foods' for your exam student. All the family can benefit from the above listed foods on a daily basis. In order to have consistency in their diet, you need to set in motion some positive habits for your child:

Consistent Persistence: Even as teenagers, you can still introduce foods to them. The secret here is to be patient and keep remembering that it usually takes twenty one days to form a new habit. It is well worth making the effort to introduce them to healthy nutrients, as this will set them up for life. Again, the secret is consistent persistence.

Set an example: As you know well, setting an example is a great way to influence your children. If you don't have greens on your plate, you can't expect your children to. Introducing them to the various arrays of vegetables at an early stage in life is setting a great example for your children. An idea is to help them cultivate a little garden patch. This gives them an appreciation of where foods come from and their links to the earth. I did this in primary school and even though slugs laced into my watercress half the time, our teacher passed on a great knowledge of food origin and that it needed to be nurtured properly to enhance its quality. You need to create a positive light around nutritious and healthy foods from a young age. If you skip breakfast or eat unhealthy snacks all the time, you are sending that message to your children, so be sure to try and set a good example and keep the messages clear and consistent.

Cook and eat together: Cooking together is a great way of show ing your children how to get into good food habits. Preparing home cooked foods is teaching them excellent life skills for their futures and it is never too late to introduce a bit of home cooking. Try and have as many 'sit-down together' meals as possible at home, as eating together will strengthen family ties and the process of eating will be less rushed also, aiding digestion. This may not always be possible with parents and children leading busy lives, but even having a family meal over the weekend to catch up, share stories and experiences of the week is pretty good. The objective is to always try to increase their variety of healthy foods. I would be in favour of giving younger children every opportunity to finish their meals and using trade-offs and bargaining to help them get their greens eaten. As a parent, this is a good time to check in and see how your exam student is coping.

The Importance Of labels: Many processed foods contain added sugar which can come in the form of glucose, sucrose, maltose, corn syrup, honey, invert sugar, hydrolysed starch, and fructose. When shopping, show your child how to read food labels and even take a picture of them to transfer to their iPad/PC for a closer look later. Educate them on the significance of the first few ingredients on a product label being the highest content ingredient in that product. Draw attention to fibre, sugar and saturated fat content on labels. At an early age, it is highly advisable to minimise your child's consumption of added sugar in order to prevent diabetes, heart problems and obesity in later life. Chapter Six contains plenty of sensible nutritional information for your perusal.

Making Meals Count

As mentioned above, I think there are huge benefits to setting meals at regular times during the day and sitting down together as a family. Mealtimes are an opportunity for families to chat, bond, discuss, ask for help and solve problems but more importantly, they are a time for eating good healthy home cooked food, like our mothers used to make. If you can spare thirty minutes out of your day, home cooked unprocessed food can be beneficial to all the family. It is also a good opportunity for an exam student to switch off from the books and give the brain a well-deserved break. The following is some guidance around food choices and making the most of family sit down meals (with exam time in focus):

Enjoyable meals: Making mealtime's fun is about being relaxed, staying calm and enjoying time together. Children will be more likely to eat if they find you in good form at the table. Eating separately or on your own in front of the TV is not ideal. Planning ahead helps greatly so that you know what's going to be cooked, who is having what and what time roughly you will all sit down together. Many parents have problems introducing new foods as children can get very attached to burgers and chips etc. You can make chicken breast or pizzas with healthy toppings together to show them that good wholesome food can be made at home too. Getting your children cooking is a great way to help them appreciate food, similar to my garden patch cultivation idea from earlier.

Notice efforts: The trick with children in any environment is to praise them when they make a genuine effort to do something, even if they don't achieve total success. Rewarding your children for good eating is something they will appreciate and remember. It's a great idea to comment on how well they did with a certain food at the end of each meal. This will create a positive attitude around that food going forward. Again this can be done at any age.

Clever choices: I think it is important to involve children in food shopping so they can choose some of their own favourite foods. They will be more likely to eat the foods at the dinner table if they have been involved in the buying process themselves. Giving them a choice between two healthy food options in the supermarket is a nice trick to ensure a healthier trolley. Buying nutritious foods when children are hungry is another psychological trick that you could try. That one is slightly more evil than the former though!

Water: Try and get your children to drink plenty of glasses of water during the day to combat dehydration. Putting a slice of orange or lemon in it will make it more interesting for them. The earlier in the day that they begin ingesting water, the better. Hydration is an extremely important element of nutrition as is fully explained in Chapter Six.

Cravings: Intense concentration and stress can leave students craving sweet treats even more. To avoid blood sugar dips and dives, choose high in cocoa, low in sugar dark chocolate. This will satisfy that sweet craving and give them an antioxidant mood boost at the same time.

Brain food: Avocados are rated in the top echelons for brain function.

They are packed with monounsaturated fats which improve blood supply to the brain, bringing oxygen and vital nutrients. A quarter to half an avocado a day is enough to reap these benefits. Blueberries are also an antioxidant powerhouse and a great stress buster, as are other dark berries like blackberries. Fresh berries can be expensive, so choose the frozen variety for a more budget friendly option.

Mixing, stacking: How food is presented on a plate to a child could influence how successful you are in promoting certain foods. When I was young, my parents found that mixing or stacking foods together worked well. Arranging foods in certain shapes or using colour makes a plate more appealing. Believe me, this is not just for younger children, as the exam child can be just as particular about how their food is presented. Try and come up with ingenious ways of making food more interesting and meals more fun. You have everything to gain!

Positively Reinforcing your Child

I would be of the school of thought that the child has to do something good before being praised and wouldn't be a massive fan of the 'Everyone gets a medal' mentality i.e. Praise for the sake of praise. However, I have seen many students' confidence flourish even after the smallest remark from an adult and I am a firm believer in positively reinforcing a person's confidence after they do something good; you then see them using this confidence to take on new challenges and further Educational and developmental successes often follow. Reinforcing your child's confidence as a reward is an excellent way of boosting their self-belief. Here is some guidance in relation to this:

Encourage their strengths: Look at school reports sent home and give them praise for the subjects they have excelled in. You need to make this the focus of your attention, rather than their shortcomings. If there is a subject that they show a skill or interest in, encourage and praise them on it, as it might end up being their career path. The last ten days prior to the exams is not the time to hound them about studying, even if they haven't been doing enough up to that point. Do remember that the strengths you used to navigate the exams all those years ago could be different to what your child draws on now.

Encourage learning In terms of their weaker subjects, if you encourage your child's love of learning, their grades should start to pick up. If you are concerned about their performance in a certain area, you could gently try to work at home with them on it. This doesn't mean forcing them to do extra work, but rather, guide them during homework to help them learn more about the subject. Practical steps like introducing the subject into everyday life can really enrich your child's education and development. This is discussed in detail (for a sample subject like Maths) in Chapter Eight. If you are unable to help them, encourage them to either collaborate with their friends or seek advice from their teacher.

Encourage ownership It is important that you allow your child to have a positive association with education. It is better to educate your child to be happy than rich, so sometimes letting them make their own decisions can be a positive. If their education is motivated by adults pressuring them or a fear of failure, it creates an unhealthy, negative vibe around learning which may lead to long term problems. I believe that a parent needs to let their secondary school child make many of their own choices. For example, this might be choosing whether to do Transition Year or picking their own subjects to do for Leaving Certificate.

My Child is Doing Exams

You are now in the situation where your child is preparing for a Junior/Leaving Cert exam and at times you probably feel you will be sitting the paper yourself. Firstly, getting stressed out and worked up will only make them more anxious. Students need to be encouraged and rewarded and this will be your main role around exam time. Getting annoyed or even angry with your child for not studying or putting in the hours will achieve very little. The only person you are annoying is yourself. The adage 'You can lead a horse to water but you can't make them drink' is apt here. As a parent, all you can do is put the conditions in place to help them flourish. Purchasing some revision books, making healthy food, providing a quiet house for study and plenty of love and support are all positive actions of an 'exam parent'.

You need to be aware that Orals and Practicals will arrive after Christmas and you will see your child's work rate intensify and maybe their stress levels also. Some of these assessments are worth a fairly substantial part of their final grade (in certain subjects) and I expect this percentage and workload to increase in the future. I guess the key here is: Awareness of what is coming up; knowing the dates, judging the difficulty by listening and just supporting them in general, without upsetting their routine.

Let them breathe

Try not to let uncertainties or worries you had in school, especially any negative vibes you had around exams, influence how your child deals with their final year. I don't think conversations like "When I was doing the Leaving Cert..." are really that helpful. Never compare your child's performance or study ethic to that of their peers, as this just adds to the stress. Complaining about the unfairness of the exam process or content appearing on specific papers is also airing unhelpful negativity. Keep it all on a positive plane and let them breathe.

With a wide variety of subjects now available in secondary school, it is inevitable that some students will experience issues with certain ones. These issues tend to circulate around a lack of confidence or a bad experience the student may have had at primary level. If you as a parent can bring the subject into the everyday life of your child and make their experiences around it more fun, classes in school will become much more manageable and interesting for them. See Chapter Eight for more information on how you can help them overcome barriers in subjects they find difficult. If you have any concerns at all about your child, you should contact their school, as teachers and management are usually more than happy to help. Similarly, if you child has a grievance or concern, it is important to go in and get the full facts of the story before making an assessment of the situation.

One of your main roles around exams is to create a good atmosphere at home and it will be important to remain calm and try not to transfer additional pressure on to your child in the lead up to them. I would be wary of placing any extra emphasis on them achieving certain grades or points. Being there for them to talk, actively listening to them and keeping career options and results in perspective are other good characteristics of the perfect 'exam parent'. I suppose it's important to guard against what they perceive as failure; support instead of policing is the way to go. To me failure in school is not about grades; the students that fail are those who don't try and the same philosophy could be applied to life. From this point of view, encouraging all their efforts is the ideal standpoint for any parent.

Anxiety and Your Child

There are lots of different ways to help your son or daughter remain calm as the exams approach. In my opinion, the best way to promote calm is to talk to them about their fears and what is going on for them. In particular, it can really help if you can get them to identify their anxious thoughts and how they are affecting them. They might explain emotions such as, "I worry I will fail and then feel sick" or they might say "I'm worried I'll forget everything".

If you find they need more than talking, ask them to write down their thoughts and concerns on a sheet of paper. Having kept a diary for ten years as a child, I found that writing down thoughts and feelings helped to get them out of my head and deal with reality better. An idea might be to ask them to write down some positive actions also, such as "I will chill and perform well" or "when I get the first question on the first paper started, I know I will feel so much better". More than any other time in their life, it is important to help your child manage their feelings, as they may struggle with overwhelming emotions and pressures placed on them by exams. There are lots of great techniques you can show them, like relaxing their breathing or helping them become aware of their feelings. If you can show them some simple techniques well before the exams arrive, they will have the opportunity to practice them beforehand.

Exercise and activities are brilliant stress reducing techniques and should be strongly encouraged. Cycling, Running, Walking, Swimming, Team Sports and Athletics are all excellent stress busters and antidotes to the anxieties exams bring. Eating well, relaxing, and good sleep routines, as discussed in previous chapters, all add constructively to their wellbeing.

You should get in touch with school if you are overly concerned about your child's anxiety, as sometimes it can happen that teachers are not aware of issues with students, and being informed, they can take steps to help them or at least cut them some slack in class. Have a read of Chapter Four for more useful tips (for both you and your child) on coping with anxiety, exam tension and techniques that bring calm. Ultimately, if you feel exam anxiety (or any other serious anxiety for that matter) is reaching an uncontrollable level, you need to seek advice, support, and guidance, probably from a medical practitioner.

Homework and Your Child

Homework is an extremely important part of your child's learning in Sixth year. See Chapter Nine for advice from existing and former students on the importance of homework. Below are some helpful tips that will hopefully facilitate your involvement in making homework a positive learning experience for your child:

- ♣ Provide your child with a suitable place and time to do their homework. Minimise interruptions/distractions from TV and other siblings.

- ♣ If a child has difficulty with homework, you should try where possible to help them overcome it with explanations and examples, without actually doing it for them.

- ♣ In the case of recurring homework problems, it is advisable to ring or send a quick note to the teacher to explain what the problem/issue is. If you are a parent of a sixth-year student, a phone call is probably the recommended form of communication.

- ♣ Parents should communicate with teachers about homework in the following cases: when your child cannot do homework due to family circumstances, when your child cannot do homework due to a lack of understanding after studying their class notes or when your child is spending an unreasonable amount of time doing homework.

♣ As well as showing an interest in their homework, you should try and link it to everyday life by regularly talking to them about sports, prices, trends, media headlines, countries, travel etc.

♣ Reward an improvement (no matter how small) in their homework with a treat. Similarly, if the teacher has made a positive note about it in their journal, a reward is well appreciated, for example: A takeaway meal/their favourite snack.

♣ Ask the Career Guidance Teacher about upcoming study skills courses which may help your child overcome any barriers in relation to homework.

♣ Talk to them about the homework they are doing in each subject. Most of all, if they are finding homework difficult, encourage them to talk to their teacher about what they find tough.

♣ If they are finding a particular type of homework difficult, encourage them to persevere, try again and maybe write down what they are finding difficult so that the teacher can see evidence of their efforts. This can help the teacher work out which learning styles suit them.

♣ Teacher's comments written on homework, class tests and mocks will help you understand what they may be doing wrong. Much of the information they learn in school applies to everyday life, so even though you may not be an expert on a subject matter, you will still be able to draw on your life experiences to tie in with what they are learning. Do not be afraid to try things or introduce perceived links with school work to your children.

♣ Make sure to check their journals regularly for comments on homework. Sixth years in particular will not like this, but it will help you keep on top of things and identify any challenges your child might be experiencing.

♣ If family circumstances change, make sure to inform the school as this can have an impact on your child's homework and performance, which the school may not be aware of.

♣ Knowing how your child is progressing in the classroom can help you make informed decisions about helping or giving them space at home. Ask the teacher to send you a homework progress comment or the odd test result home in their journal, in order to keep up to date with each subject.

♣ Attending Parent-teacher meetings is really important during your child's exam year, so plan ahead to make yourself available for these when the annual school calendar is released. You can use this as an opportunity to discuss progress and how your child is coping with homework. It also serves to show your child that you have a keen interest in how they are progressing in various subjects. In my experience, it is good to enhance communication links with your child's teachers, as your child is now aware that a communication line has been established between two important people in their life.

Parenting on Exam Days

Your first job as a parent around exam time is to maintain normality, so try to preserve the habits and timings that you have developed at home during term time, right up until the end of the exams. This will help your child maintain their own habits and patterns; something teenagers crave. Daily patterns we engage in include rising, eating, leisure time, and sleeping. Routine, pattern and consistency will help maintain balance for your child on exam days and allow them to flourish in the exam hall.

You should keep perspective and be realistic for your child, advising them to do so also. I have seen some situations where students lock themselves in their rooms on an almost twenty-hour study buzz. If you are a parent in that situation, you should encourage your child to take breaks via a balanced Lifestyle Timetable as I have previously proposed. Even a brisk twenty minute walk can work wonders. You are the expert on your own child and will know if the volume of study they are taking on is affecting them personally.

Above all, ensure they are getting at least eight hours sleep a night on exam days. If they are struggling to sleep, you may consider a magnesium supplement from the health store, which helps calm the nervous system aiding sleep. Keep an eye on your child's caffeine intake. Some studies suggest that small amounts of coffee increases alertness. Other studies say that taking excess caffeine can upset our blood sugars affecting concentration. Either way, caffeine may play havoc with sleep patterns, so reducing intake to a maximum of one to two cups a day is sensible, abstaining after four p.m. Energy drinks are strongly discouraged. (See Chapter Six for more information on nutrition).

Many teenagers have issues contextualising situations and struggle to see the bigger picture, so emphasis on them doing their best at any given moment will go a long way. You may feel helpless if they don't open up to you, but try and understand their motivation and what's in it for them to work really hard. Ask them what they want out of it and speak with them about their hopes and goals, in order to get a better understanding of the situation.

Go For It: Advise

It is good to talk to your child about unpredictability before the first exam, in case they are adopting an 'eggs in one basket' philosophy to some exam papers. Reassure them in relation to the levels they have chosen in certain subjects and advise them to hang in there if they see something unfamiliar on the paper, as often questions are not as bad as they seem when first read. The reality is that something unfamiliar is probably that to thousands of other kids too, so they are not alone. Most importantly, talk to your child about remaining calm when they receive their exam paper, as a small amount of them press the panic button and draw a complete blank. You will know yourself if your child is likely to do this, so encouraging them to take a few seconds out, a sip of water, a few deep breaths and read the question again, is the best advice you can give them here.

You might also speak to them about the importance of marking schemes. You don't need to be familiar with how each paper is corrected and they will more than likely know how marking schemes work at this stage. However, it is worth reminding them that it is relatively easy to pick up attempt marks for what they know. Remind them also that really difficult papers tend to be marked a little easier and if paper one goes badly in a subject, paper two usually tends to work out better. I have heard of students giving up on a subject because paper one went badly, the most common comment being "I failed my Leaving Cert". Your role here is to pick them up mentally for paper two, convincing them that it is literally only 'half-time'.

Exam Day Parenting-Reference Guide

Every day during the exams, your child will need renewed encouragement from you, which they will draw strength from. Here is a quick reference advice list for parenting on exam day:

- ♣ Offer support and encouragement.

- ♣ Advise them to avoid caffeine.

- ♣ Stock up on nuts, seeds, fruit, and vegetables.

- ♣ Try to be more of a coach than a parent.

- ♣ Prepare whatever food they may need on the day of the exams.

- ♣ De-clutter their room if they would like you to.

- ♣ Remain calm, as your child will pick up on your anxiety.

- ♣ Give them belief in themselves.

- ♣ Let them vent if they need to.

- ♣ Tell them regularly "I'm so proud of you" and "you are working so well".

- ♣ Encourage exercise, sleep and taking breaks.

- ♣ Remind them that this exam will not determine their life.

- ♣ Help them to get the work-study balance correct.

- ♣ Try not to overstate the importance of their exams.

- ♣ Give them space to breathe.

- ♣ Ask them what support and help they need around exam time, not the other way around.

♣ Sit down with them and see what their plan is. Ask them can you help in any way.

♣ Encourage regular breaks from studying, as no one can concentrate for hours on end.

♣ Keep your expectations realistic remembering it is your child, not you that is sitting the exam.

♣ Try to keep your emotions stable over the exam period.

Stability=Routine=Familiarity=Calmness=Good Performance

♣ If they need to talk to you, let them talk, otherwise space and support is what's required.

♣ Look out for the big efforts they are putting in and reward them with munchies or a fun trip.

♣ Be fully aware that exams may be an anxious time for them. There are plenty of students who have trouble eating and sleeping due to anxiety over exams. As a result, writing an exam paper may be difficult for them.

♣ Set up a quiet comfortable environment for study. If possible, setup a study area outside their bedroom so that the anxiety and stress of studying is not associated with sleep. Ensure their study and relaxation areas are clearly demarcated. Try and keep your home free of distractions and the atmosphere as calm as possible.

If you are concerned about how your child is coping before or during the exams, it is advisable to contact your doctor or the school guidance counsellor.

What if They Have a Bad Exam Day?

Most Leaving Cert students will be sitting seven plus subjects in their exams with Junior Cycle students sitting up to twelve. Your child will have a picture in their head of how they think each exam will pan out for them, but unfortunately it is never that simple. The SEC is increasingly trying to make the exams unpredictable and so surprises will occur. It is how your child deals with these surprises that will determine how well they perform.

Supporting your child as they prepare for their exams is essential in helping them cope with exam stress. It is a stressful time for even the most organised and intelligent student but stressing over their stress is not going to help anyone. The likelihood is that over the two weeks, at least one exam will not go exactly to plan and if you can help them during this tough time, it will be much appreciated. If things go wrong and they have a bad day, you should encourage them to take a nice long break and cook them a nice meal.

It is a good idea to check-in every day to see how things are going, even with subjects they are feeling confident about. You know your child better than anyone so keep an eye out for signals of poor confidence and down times. Car journeys can be a good time to tap into how they are feeling about current or upcoming exams. Even during exam time, separating 'family' and 'social media' time is a good ploy to keep the chat lines open and establish clear boundaries. Good communication is really important around exam time, especially if your child is shy or not a talker.

If they tell you an exam didn't go well, ask them why they thought it didn't. They are very likely to say "you wouldn't understand" which is fine, but there are many words of comfort and encouragement you can give them. Try to work through their anxieties without asking a million questions and interrogating them; from experience, parents can be guilty of this without even knowing. Let them feel like they are in control and do not judge any observations or concerns they may have. The "I told you so" or "Well you should have studied harder" lines aren't really going to help things. You need to continue to support and reassure them about how well they are doing and that tomorrow will be better, even if you are feeling as anxious and nervous as they are. You are their role model and they will always look up to you (even if they don't always give that impression).

From a technical point of view, unless you are a subject teacher, you are more than likely not going to analyse the paper they have just completed. Let them vocally analyse it if they need to and hopefully this will benefit them mentally for their next exam. Negative feedback afterwards is futile since the exam is over and you are just raking over something they can't change anyway. They will probably be aware of the errors they have made and hopefully, they can learn from them. After going through this process with your child using interventions you deem suitable, you need to show your confidence and belief in them now. You have seen how hard your child worked during the year, what teachers have said about them and what they have scored in their class tests, so make sure and remind them of those successes, showing you still believe in them.

At seventeen/eighteen, not many of us knew what we wanted to do in life. The expectations on teenagers today to know what they want to do, even before they get their results, is high. Some go to college, some take a year out, some defer, some repeat, some go straight into the work place, but some also lose their way. As a parent, you signed up to raising a happy and healthy child and anything else is a bonus. Most of us adults aren't doing what we set out to do after our Leaving Certificate, so we need to let our children develop their own careers during the various twists and turns of life.

In summary the three P's will greatly soothe a bad day in the exam hall: Positivity, Praise and Providing treats. These will divert their mind and break the cycle of self-pity. Telling them how proud you are of all their efforts is the best you can do in any situation.

Message to My Wonderful Daughter

Ultimately, they need to know that you are there for them with your unconditional care and support. The strength of this support is so obvious in the emotion I hear from speaking to parents about their children each week. This emotion was very evident in a post a friend of mine put up on Social media for her daughter the night before the Leaving Cert results this year. I thought it was a great way of showing her that life was more important than results and that she wouldn't ultimately be defined by them. It went as follows:

> *"The very best of luck to all the students receiving their exam results tomorrow. I actually cannot sleep and then having to wait until next week to find out about college places and if she's been an especially amazing daughter is hard. My princess has bought pots and pans and what not for her third level accommodation. So, could everyone please just say a few decades of the rosary for her or an auld candle will suffice.*

No matter how you do my precious girl, I'm one proud momma. So very proud of the beautiful young lady you have become so far. You are so beautiful in more ways than one. You are smart, funny, intelligent, my #indigochild, and kind. Sometimes too kind for your own good. But I still wouldn't change a single thing about you. Every single strand of hair on your precious head is so very special and so very precious to me. You were put here to make the world a little bit brighter and you certainly make all our lives so much so. I don't need you to get 'x' amount of points to know that you are capable of doing anything you want to do. I don't need to measure your intelligence based on how many points you get tomorrow. All our paths are, to some extent, already paved out for us. We all know right from wrong and you have good morals which have and always will serve you well. Best of luck for tomorrow. I hope you get the points you are expecting and there's nothing wrong with repeating. As long as you're happy that's all that matters to me baby girl."

Paula Bhreathnach (Parent of Leaving Cert Student)

College Applications

If your child underachieves in their exams, they may not get their first Central Applications Office (CAO) choice but they could still be in with a shot at getting their second or third. Additionally, they will have time, when the exams are over, to reconsider their CAO options and change them. Prior to all of this, it is important to remind them to put down courses in their order of preference on the CAO form. If there is a course they really want to do but think they won't get the points for it, make sure they put it down on the form anyway, as much can happen in a few months and they could well surprise themselves. The other thing you need to remind them to do is to check if there is a minimum grade required in a specific subject for entry to their course. If they don't meet a grade requirement, no matter how many points they get, they will not get their place on that course. An example of this could be a 'pass' grade in a certain subject. There are other routes they can take, external to the CAO process and the career guidance teacher is the first port of call for advice here.

If you or your child are struggling with the CAO form, you should contact their school, and staff members will be more than happy to help. It is important that your child is realistic about the options that are available to them. Of course it would be fantastic if everyone got their first choice, but there are always possibilities via second or third choices too. I wouldn't be choosing a university based on the fact that their friends are going there and remember that college is not for everyone. One hundred points can be worth more to a student than six hundred to another, so irrespective of ability, if they put the work in, they will reap the rewards in their own way. They will find a life path.

Final Tips for Guiding your Child Through the Exams

Here are my final tips for being an amazingly supportive parent during the exams. Hopefully you will be able to draw on some of them when the time comes:

Know their timetable: Pin the exam timetable up prominently at home; highlight each exam your child will sit. Put the date and time of each paper into your diary or calendar. You need to be continuously aware of when they should be in the examination centre. For parents who are working and leaving home early in the morning, avoid the disaster of your child missing an exam. Ensure they are up and dressed before you leave home for work. A small number of students fail to turn up for morning papers and they will not be admitted thirty minutes after exam start time.

Encourage final checks: Help them to draw up a check list of daily requirements based on the next day's exams. Encourage them to make a final check on equipment each morning before they leave home. Writing instruments along with the other requirements such as rulers, erasers, calculators, water, and any non-intrusive nourishment such as glucose sweets or fruit should be checked for inclusion.

Listen: When your child arrives home after the day, listen to their experience carefully and then move on. After each day's exams allow them to talk through their experience of it. Do not be tempted to review any errors or omissions on the paper with them. Such a process achieves absolutely nothing, other than to increase a student's stress levels. Allow them the time and space to tell their tale and move on to the challenge of the next paper.

Awareness: It can be helpful if you have a little knowledge of the next upcoming paper or at least be able to show some interest in it. Simple questions such as, "What is up next?", "Are there any compulsory sections?" or "Are there any predictable questions?" can be asked. These questions may be useful in helping your child devise their lifestyle timetable (See Chapter Two) for the next few days.

Recharge: Help them maintain a well-balanced daily routine. You should ensure your child strikes a proper balance between study and rest. After an exam, they need time to rest and recharge before they can do any worthwhile study for the next paper. Remember that on average, the exams are a two-week process and students need to be as sharp on the morning of their final paper as they are on the first. Late-night study sessions are not advised.

Sleep is good: Studies have shown that a good night's sleep improves exam performance. All study should end at least an hour before bedtime to allow your child time to unwind before sleep. Encourage them to wind down body and mind to promote a refreshing night's sleep. There are many breathing apps on smartphones now that you can download to help. It is not advisable to fall straight into bed from the study desk as their mind will be buzzing for hours as they attempt to get to sleep. You can advise them appropriately on these matters. Sleeping should be encouraged, so maybe set an example by going to bed early yourself during this period. Phone use before sleep is not good.

Solid nutrition: As I have already touched on, whatever children eat and drink has a big effect on their body but more importantly it affects performance in activities. This is especially pertinent in activities involving mental sharpness. As a parent, you should try to ensure your child consumes nutritious food during the coming weeks; starting with breakfast each morning; the lunch they bring with them, if they are facing two exams; their evening meal; as well as snacks during the day. Grazing on junk food is very tempting at times of increased stress but should be avoided at all costs. See Chapter Six for more information on eating around exam time and general nutrition for your child.

Positivity: Drawing on the support of everything that is potentially positive in a student's life helps to maximise exam performance. Other family members need to be fully aware of how they can help the exam student. Helping to maintain a student's high spirits during the extended exam period is worth its weight in gold. Be a good listener and let them tell you things as they will, be that moaning or delighting. Your challenge is to try and keep them on an even keel, not getting too up if things go well or too down if disaster strikes. Focus on the positives and always encourage.

Believe in them: It is worth remembering that the Leaving Cert is much hyped, more than it should be. Friends and family can unknowingly hype it with comments and chit chat. We have learned to live with this hype over the years as it further embeds itself into Irish culture. The media spotlight will be more pronounced before the first day as they search for spins to fill newspaper and online columns. To guard against this; encourage your child to stick with their plan and keep believing in themselves. It is important for you not to hype any examination, since it is very easy in the middle of a stress-induced experience, such as a major exam, to get the whole event out of perspective. You should ensure your child is clear that your unconditional care and support for them is in no way dependent on how they perform in the Leaving Certificate. Your affirmation of the type of person they are is greater than any set of amazing results.

ACE Inspirational Quotes

—————— ♥ ♠ ♦ ♣ ——————

"Imagination is more important than knowledge"
Albert Einstein.

"Where the needs of the world and your talents cross,
there lies your vocation"
Aristotle.

The Chequered Flag is in Sight...

I have enjoyed imparting my experience and knowledge to you through this book and am confident that you now have a useful resource to draw on at any time during your final year in school. To me, it all comes back to two things; belief in yourself and smart, hard work.

When you were a young child, you told everyone how wonderful you were and what you were going to be in life; you never sold yourself short. Soon you will be an adult, so don't sell yourself short then either. Keep believing in what you really want from life and have confidence in your qualities and talents.

I have never met a hard worker that was unsuccessful and if you possess the will and passion for something, there are always walls you can break down or alternate routes available to reach your goals. You are bringing so many special skills and abilities to these exams and you will graduate soon having been transformed from a rough stone into a faceted gem.

Take the risks, radiate positivity, ignore the codology and always work smart in pursuit of that winning hand. Go in there and own it.

ACE the Leaving Cert!

Appendix

"Being Exam Smart"- Survey of Leaving Certificate Students*

1. What are the important things to do around exam time?

2. What are important things not to do around exam time?

3. How are you going to go about studying as the exams near?

4. What advice would you give to third year students?

5. If you could get hold of information from someone to advise you about exams, what information would be helpful to you?

6. What parts of doing exams do you struggle with?

7. What three pieces of advice would you give younger students, i.e. First, second and third years doing class exams in May?

8. Name something that would have been really helpful before your last exam?

9. List some things you found important about homework?

10. List seven tips you would give to someone preparing for exams?

11. What would you say to Junior Cycle students about how to handle the pressure and do the right thing in the exam hall?

12. What mistakes did you feel you made just before the Junior Cycle exam and inside the exam hall on the day? You can include issues in class or mock exams.

*Cohort of Sixty Students Surveyed.

Bibliography

Center for disease control and prevention: National Health and Nutrition Survey of America, Center for disease control and prevention, 2012, United States of America.

Dr. P. Mannix McNamara: Why Education Should Flourish (Blog), 2016, Ireland – Accessed May 2017.

E. Dale: Theory into Practice– Adapted from Edgar Dale Audio (Visual method in Teaching), Taylor and Francis ltd, 1970, United   States of America.

http://www.bodywhys.ie – Accessed June 2017.
http://www.diabetes.ie – Accessed June 2017.
http://www.open.ac.uk – Accessed June 2017.

J. Bradley, F. Keane, S. Crawford: School Sport and Academic Achievement, American School Health Association, 2013, United States of America.

N. Collins: Article on Fluid and Food for Sport: via website http://www.nevergiveup.ie, 2015, Ireland.

P. Holford and J. Burne: Food is Better Medicine than Drugs, Piatkus, 2017, Great Britain.

CPSIA information can be obtained
at www.ICGtesting.com
Printed in the USA
LVHW101405240521
688335LV00024B/1266

9 781724 480507